Robert Fulton

Robert Fulton

PIONEER OF
UNDERSEA WARFARE

BY WALLACE HUTCHEON, JR.

NAVAL INSTITUTE PRESS
Annapolis, Maryland

Printed in the United States of America

Library of Congress Cataloging in Publication Data
Hutcheon, Wallace, Jr., 1933-
    Robert Fulton: Pioneer of Undersea Warfare
    Bibliography: p.
    Includes index.
    Supt. of Docs. no.: D 201.2:F95
    1. Fulton, Robert, 1765-1815. 2. Naval art and
    science. 3. Naval architects—United States—
    Biography. I. Title.
    VM140.F9H87   623.8'25'0924 [B]   80-81094
    ISBN 0-87021-547-7

To the Hutcheon Ladies
and
To the Memory of My Father

Contents

Acknowledgments   ix

Introduction   xi

Prologue   The "War of 1807"   1

1   The Young Artist At Home and Abroad   4

2   The French Connection, 1797–1803   18

3   A Sojourn in Britain, 1804–1806   62

4   Homecoming, 1807–1814   93

5   "Fulton the First"   127

Robert Fulton and Naval Warfare   149

Notes   154

Bibliography   170

Index   188

Acknowledgments

On the morning of 15 November 1966, the late Wood Gray, Professor of History at George Washington University, began his class with a deeply felt plea for a new "treatment" of Robert Fulton. Professor Gray's request marked the genesis of my interest in Fulton, and this book is the result. For the next ten years, this dedicated scholar nurtured my interest and guided my research on Fulton in various graduate reading courses and seminars. My greatest regret is that Professor Gray did not live to see the finished work.

I owe a great debt to Peter P. Hill, also a Professor of History at George Washington University. Professor Hill saw me through the pitfalls and challenges of developing my theme as a doctoral dissertation. One of these challenges included airmailing chapters across the Atlantic Ocean while Professor Hill was engaged in research in Paris. He returned the chapters with most helpful comments so quickly that my fears of delay were soon obviated. Thanks to a great degree to his guidance, the dissertation was accepted by George Washington University in 1975.

In addition, I would like to express my appreciation to the following individuals for their aid, encouragement, and support:

Professor Charles P. Poland, Jr., Professor of History at

Northern Virginia Community College, my immediate supervisor for most of the past decade and my friend always;

Dr. Howard M. Merriman, former Professor of History, George Washington University;

Dr. Philip K. Lundeberg, Curator of Naval History, Museum of History and Technology, Smithsonian Institution;

Dr. Alex Roland, Assistant Historian, National Aeronautics and Space Administration;

Alan D. Frazer, Curator/Registrar, the New Jersey Historical Society.

I owe a special debt of gratitude to Eve Fritz, who typed the manuscript in its final form, and I would also like to thank Linda Miller and Anne Wilson, who worked on its early stages of development.

Appreciation is also due to the staff of the Naval Institute Press, and especially to Deborah Guberti, whose enthusiasm and support for the project made the author-editor connection a most pleasant one.

I would like to acknowledge the aid received in research by the staffs of the New-York Historical Society, New York Public Library, New Jersey Historical Society, Historical Society of Pennsylvania, Columbia University Library, Library of Congress, U.S. National Archives, Navy Department Library, Smithsonian Institution, and the Naval Academy Museum.

Finally, special mention must be made of my wife Margaret and my daughters Dorothy Lee and Hillary Ann. They did absolutely no work on the project, but without their love and encouragement the book would never have been completed.

Introduction

Although best known for his construction of the steamboat, Robert Fulton was a man whose interests and talents were amazingly diverse. In addition to his work on the steamboat, he was a painter, a canal engineer and promoter, a sometime philosopher and passing fair writer, and even for a time a showman. He also played a very important role in the field of naval warfare, his accomplishments in this area including the development of the submarine, the mine, mine warfare tactics, an underwater cannon, an anchor cutter, a primitive proto-type of the patrol torpedo boat, troop transport, and the first steam warship. He himself recognized the importance of his work in this field. He believed, in fact, that his naval inventions would ultimately be more significant than the steamboat. An even greater American, President Thomas Jefferson, agreed with this assessment.

This study will not attempt to address in any great detail Fulton's role in the invention of the steamboat. Of all the works that have been written on this subject, James Thomas Flexner's *Steamboats Come True: American Inventors in Action,* originally published in 1944 and reissued in 1978, is by far the most impressive. It is both scholarly and a pleasure to read.

Rather, the primary purpose of this study is to describe and evaluate both the scope and significance of Robert Fulton's work in the area of naval warfare. Representing a synthesis of past studies on this subject as well as an analysis of source materials, many of which were previously undiscovered, this book should show that Robert Fulton's work in the field of naval warfare was more significant than most have realized.

The book is divided into four parts in broad chronological order, each of which describes Fulton's achievements in one of the three countries in which he resided during his life. Preceded by a summary of his early life, the first phase of the book describes how Fulton began his work in the field of naval warfare in 1797 in France with his submarine project. The second phase of the book discusses Fulton's developing theory of and experimentation with "torpedo" war, really the genesis of modern mine warfare, while he was in England from 1804 to 1806. The last two phases of the book consider his work in the United States from 1807 until his death in 1815, the third phase describing his experiments with "torpedo" war and the use of his invention during the War of 1812, the fourth phase examining his development and construction of the first steam warship in history.

Both phases three and four will describe and analyze Robert Fulton's association with the United States Navy. Stressed will be Fulton's relationships with Presidents Jefferson and Madison, naval secretaries Robert Smith, Paul Hamilton, and especially William Jones, and key naval officers including Commodore John Rodgers and Captain Stephen Decatur. A description and assessment of Fulton's bid to become Madison's secretary of the Navy in 1814 will be included in the fourth phase.

Finally, to what extent Fulton's naval concepts and experiments affected later developments in naval warfare will be briefly examined. Just as the steamboat appears to have had a greater effect on the nineteenth century than on the century following it, a case can be made that Fulton's naval innovations and philosophies would have greater impact on the twentieth century than on the nineteenth.

Robert Fulton

Prologue
The "War of 1807"

It was the summer of 1807. After a twenty-year extended sojourn in Europe, Robert Fulton had recently returned to America. The forty-two-year-old artist and inventor had spent almost all of his adult life away from his native land. In just a few weeks, in September, he would gain immortality with his steamboat voyage up the Hudson River. However, in July of 1807, Robert Fulton was courting fame (or disaster) in another area. He had conceived and proposed a unique naval operation against ships of the Royal Navy. If his scheme had been accepted and put into effect, and it was seriously considered by those in authority, it might well have precipitated war with Great Britain at that time.

Robert Fulton's naval plan was a response to the famous encounter between the USS *Chesapeake* and HMS *Leopard*. On 22 June 1807, the American frigate *Chesapeake* was intercepted by the heavier-gunned British frigate *Leopard* a few miles off the Virginia capes. The British commander of naval forces in North America, Vice Admiral George Berkeley, had ordered his ships to stop American naval vessels in order to search for British deserters. After a brief, most then believed too brief, exchange of gunfire, the *Chesapeake* hove to, and her commanding officer permitted the British to remove four seamen. The American ship returned to Norfolk in disgrace and for several weeks the nation expected a conflict with Britain. On 7 July, President Jefferson wrote to Secretary of War Henry Dearborn, "The British commanders have their foot on the threshold of war. They have begun the blockade of Norfolk."[1] Jefferson was extremely fearful of a possible British attack on the *Chesapeake* and other American vessels moored in Hampton Roads. He ordered Dearborn to go to New York and observe that city's plans for harbor defense. President Jefferson concluded his directive with the key words, "I am in hopes you will also see Fulton's experiment tried and see how far his means may enter into our plan."[2] The president referred to a naval weapons demonstration that Robert Fulton had scheduled in New York for later in July in order to prove that his naval mines were capable of destroying warships. Secretary of War Dearborn arrived in New York on 11 July and immediately began investigating the harbor defense situation.[3] When he heard of the British threat to Norfolk, Robert Fulton proposed a new and startling scheme to Dearborn, who passed it on to Secretary of State James Madison:

> Fulton . . . is very desirous of being permitted to blow up some of the Ships that have given us so much trouble near Norfolk, he [ascertains?] no doubts of complete success. I wish those Rascals would go away and be quiett [sic] until the hot season is over, but if they will not, I think we may as well let Fulton try [some?] experiments upon them. If he could blow up one of their . . . Ships, I doubt whether any others would trouble us again. . . .[4]

As it turned out, Fulton's weapons were not necessary. On 17 July, President Jefferson wrote to Dearborn that the British fleet had departed from the Hampton Roads area.[5] Thus the immediate threat passed, and Robert Fulton did not have the opportunity to employ his "torpedos," as he called them, at this time. It was probably just as well, for if he had, the War of 1812 might have had to be renamed the "War of 1807."

Robert Fulton's proposal to blow up the British ships may be considered somewhat extreme. The reader will learn in addition that in December 1797, just months after leaving his English friends for France, Fulton proposed using his submarine to attack the Royal Navy. Then in 1804, back in

England, he offered the English the use of his naval weapons against his French comrades of the past seven years. Now, in 1807, just seven months after leaving England for the last time, he was prepared to destroy British ships. It has been said of the French statesman Talleyrand that one had to beware of his sudden vacations; whenever he left Paris in such a manner, something very serious would soon happen to the current French government. Something of the same sort can be said of Robert Fulton. Whenever he departed from a country, that country had better quickly prepare its naval defenses! The cynic might say that it was perhaps a good thing that Robert Fulton never left the United States again. Fulton, however, always remained loyal to his native land, throughout the long years of his absence, and especially after his return.

1

The Young Artist
At Home and Abroad

Naval matters played no role in the first phase of Robert Fulton's life. He was born on 14 November 1765, on a farm in Little Britain, Pennsylvania. His birthplace is located by Conowingo Creek on a crossroads in the sparsely populated region of southern Lancaster County, close to the Maryland border.

The Fulton family was of Scotch-Irish ancestry. Fulton's father, Robert Fulton, Senior, had married Mary Smith of Chester County in the 1750s. The Fultons lived in the city of Lancaster, on the northeast corner of the main square, from 1759 until 1765. In the spring of that year they moved approximately twenty miles south of town to the Little Britain farm of 393-3/4 acres where Robert was born that fall.

Very little is known of Robert Fulton and his family during this time. His father was said to have been a founder of the Presbyterian Church in Lancaster, and to have led the singing there. Although a recent demographic study of the region indicates, rather surprisingly for that time, that roughly half of the inhabitants of Little Britain township were not employed as farmers, Fulton's father chose to make his living as a farmer.[1] He was not a success at it, however, and financial problems continually plagued the family. In the winter of 1771–72, the Fultons had to leave the Little Britain farm. The elder Fulton pathetically notified the new owner: "The forth of this instent all my moveabels was sold even the Beds and . . . furnetur only our Clothing was Exceptd . . . i have Nothing to By Land Back Nor money to [word indistinct] with in town Besides it is verry Disegrable to my wife and Family to go Back, My whole Dependence is on what will arise on the seall of the place. . . ."[2] Despite this distaste for moving back to Lancaster, the Fulton family returned to the city and the father died soon thereafter.

How the widow Fulton supported Robert and his three sisters and younger brother is not known. Young Robert was sent to a school on the square in Lancaster run by a stern Quaker schoolmaster. He does not appear to have been a model student. According to Fulton's great-granddaughter and biographer, Alice Crary Sutcliffe, this teacher was beating Robert's hand with a stick one day when the future inventor allegedly said, "Sir, I came to have something beaten into my brains, and not into my knuckles." While quite possibly a fictitious

Robert Fulton's birthplace, Lancaster County, Pennsylvania

story, there is no evidence that young Fulton was very fond of "book learning." On the other hand, he seems to have had a reputation among his classmates for practical experimentation; his descendant notes that his experiments with quicksilver, which he purchased, earned him the name "Quicksilver Bob." Fulton's first interest in water transportation occurred in Lancaster County while fishing on Conestoga Creek. Not caring for the exercise of rowing or poling, he is said to have constructed a rude set of paddlewheels for the boat, to be operated manually.[3]

Robert Fulton grew up during the violent days of the American Revolution, a time when the city of Lancaster was earning increasing significance as a major gun manufacturing center in the colonies. While there is no evidence to support it, the teenage Fulton may well have been drawn to the gun shops, where he could observe the workers constructing and tinkering with the weapons. It is indeed possible that during this time he developed his interest in the machines of warfare. In 1775 the British officer John Andre, who was to earn both fame and death in 1780 because of his appointment to negotiate with Benedict Arnold for the betrayal of West Point, was captured and paroled in Lancaster. A familiar Fulton family story has the chivalrous Englishman teaching young Fulton how to paint; again no primary sources support this legend. Fulton did, however, begin to develop his talent and love for painting at this time.

Sometime before his seventeenth birthday in 1782, Fulton decided that he needed to broaden his experience as a painter and moved to Philadelphia. If we can imagine the youthful Pennsylvanian trudging eastward towards future fame and fortune, perhaps we can also appreciate the Lancastrian pride reflected in the 1909 verse by the Pennsylvania sonneteer, Lloyd Mifflin, describing one of the area's most famous native sons and his origins:

A child of Lancaster, upon this land,
Here was he born, by Conowingo's shade;
Along these banks our youthful Fulton strayed
Dreaming of Art. Then Science touched his hand,

Leading him onward, when, beneath her wind,
Wonders appeared that now shall never fade. . . .[4]

Robert Fulton stayed in Philadelphia for more than four years. He had a hard time earning a living as an artist until he was gradually able to establish himself as a painter of miniature portraits. Although apprenticed at first to a jeweler named Jeremiah Andrews, Fulton seems to have developed his artistic skills without much assistance from Andrews. At least one authority believes that Fulton's style may reflect the tutelage of the artists Charles Willson Peale or his brother James.[5]

A prosperous Philadelphia businessman, John Ross, took a liking to young Fulton and commissioned him to paint portraits of Ross's two daughters. Fulton was also supposed to have painted a representation of Benjamin Franklin, who returned home from Europe in September 1785 after negotiating the treaties with France and Britain that ended the American Revolution. Fulton may have done this painting, but if he did, its location is not presently known. Although some critics feel Fulton's later paintings are good, the known work of his Philadelphia period is not impressive. His best efforts were probably his portraits of Mr. John Wilkes Kittera, a wealthy merchant, and his wife, painted sometime in the middle of the decade and presently owned by the Historical Society of Pennsylvania.

During his years in Philadelphia, Fulton was occasionally debilitated by ill health. In 1817, the physician who had attended Fulton's final illness related the following piece of medical history: "At about eighteen or twenty years of age, in consequence of exposure to cold, Mr. Fulton was attacked with an inflammation of the lungs; this was succeeded by a spitting of blood, and other symptoms indicating a disposition of pulmonary complaints. . . ."[6] Because of his poor health, Fulton left Philadelphia temporarily in 1786 for the medicinal waters of Bath in Virginia, known today as Berkeley Springs, now in West Virginia, and located approximately 100 miles up the Potomac from Washington, D.C. Here Fulton nourished the idea of going to Europe, both for his health and to further his artistic education. He returned to Philadelphia, somehow obtained the necessary funds for the trip, as well as reference letters to important Americans living abroad, departed and arrived in London in 1787. Robert Fulton would not see the United States again for twenty years.

As it turned out, Fulton's most significant letter of introduction was to the painter Benjamin West. Known at the time as the "American Raphael" because of his similarity in style to the Renaissance artist, West was a unique individual in several respects. The first well-known American artist to be acclaimed abroad, West began the tradition of famous Americans residing in Europe; as Henry James would be to the nineteenth century and Ernest Hemingway to the twentieth, Benjamin West was to the eighteenth. Next, he was unique both as George III's court painter and as a foreign-born president of the famed Royal Academy. Finally, there was no one who trained and patronized younger American artists abroad to the extent that West did. Among those who studied under him were John Singleton Copley, Charles Willson Peale, Gilbert Stuart, John Trumbull, Samuel F.B. Morse—and Robert Fulton.

Benjamin West was born in Pennsylvania in 1738. Authorities do not agree as to whether there had been any significant contact between West and the Fulton family in Lancaster County. In any event, West lived in Philadelphia, and moved to Europe in order to study art, several years before Fulton was born. On leaving America in 1760, West went first to Italy and became the first American painter of stature to master the neoclassicist style and adapt it in paintings that reflected his native environment. West later moved to London and achieved immediate fame in 1771 with his painting *The Death of Wolfe*. After his appointment as court painter by King George III, West's reputation was secure and would remain so until his death in 1820. Joel Barlow, great friend and sponsor of Robert Fulton during his forthcoming long residency in France, would pay homage to Fulton's renowned teacher in England in his revised *Columbiad*:

> . . . West with his own great soul the canvas warms,
> Creates, inspires, impassions human forms,
> Spurns critic rules, and seizing safe the heart,
> Breaks down the former frightful bounds of Art. . . .[7]

While in London, Robert Fulton did not live in West's lodgings, residing instead for a time at Cavendish Square. However, much of Fulton's creative life was spent in the senior Pennsylvanian's London home. Leigh Hunt, an English Romantic writer, remembered today chiefly for the poems, "Abou ben Adhem" and "Jenny Kissed Me," rather mockingly recalled West in his studio:

. . . The gallery was a continuation of the house passage,
and, together with one of those rooms and the parlor,
formed three sides of a garden, very small but elegant . . .
The two rooms contained the largest of his pictures; and in
the farther one, after stepping softly down the gallery, as if
reverencing the dumb life on the walls, you generally found
the mild and quiet artist at his work; happy, for he thought
himself immortal.[8]

Fulton's and West's mutual love of painting soon developed into a firm and secure friendship. When Fulton finally returned to the United States, West gave the younger American a self-portrait showing West painting his wife. Mrs. West was also very fond of Robert Fulton and, indeed, looked upon him as an adopted son. In addition, West painted Fulton's portrait and gave it to him. The length and steadfastness of their friendship is reflected in the following 1813 Fulton letter to West: "My good friend . . . this success of your late works have added much to your fame, in which your friends here sincerely rejoice; for the mind to grow vigorous after 60 is a precious gift of nature. May she continue her favors until you shall be the oldest and most celebrated painter that ever lived."[9]

One of the most remarkable characteristics of Fulton was his ability to attract key personalities of the social and intellectual world and to form with these people, in most cases, enduring relationships. According to his American friend and first biographer, Cadwallader D. Colden, Fulton made an excellent appearance. He was approximately six feet tall and had a slender frame. Colden says: "Nature had made him a gentleman, and bestowed upon him ease and gracefulness . . . His features were strong, and of a manly beauty: he had large dark eyes, and a projecting brow, expressive of intelligence and

thought: his temper was mild, and his disposition lively. . . ."[10]
One of Fulton's strongest characteristics was that, unlike many
who profess to, he genuinely liked people: ". . . he was fond of
society, which he always enlivened by cheerful, cordial man-
ners, and instructed or pleased by his sensible conversation.
. . . In all his domestic and social relations he was zealous,
kind, generous, liberal, and affectionate. . . ."[11]

One of the most important figures of the English Industrial
Revolution was the inventor of the power loom, Edmund Cartwright. His memorialist recalls that "Mr. Fulton's vivacity of
character and original way of thinking rendered him a wel-
come guest at Mr. Cartwright's house."[12] Nearly all of Robert
Fulton's biographers have commented on Fulton's capacity for
hard work and industry. Again, his American friend Colden
has said it best, ". . . what was most conspicuous in his
character, was his calm constancy, his industry, and that in-
defatigable patience and perseverance which always enabled
him to overcome difficulties."[13]

Indeed, Robert Fulton exemplified some of the best characteristics of the Enlightenment movement. His optimism, his
belief in science and reason, and above all his interest in and
concern for a wide variety of pursuits, made him, like his ad-
mirer Thomas Jefferson, a prime model of the Enlightenment
enthusiast.

Lest it appear that Robert Fulton was unrealistically virtuous, his apparent fondness for money has also often been
stressed by biographers. While there is certainly some truth in
this, Fulton's background of poverty and his natural desire to
overcome this handicap are certainly understandable. He
never amassed a fortune and died a poor man.

Ultimately, what really stands out about Robert Fulton is his
great confidence and belief in himself. Year after year, despite
financial problems and lack of recognition, this boundless faith
in his own potential would sustain him throughout his
endeavors.

Robert Fulton's social breakthrough in England came in
1791 with an invitation to visit Devonshire, to paint the portrait of Viscount William Courtenay, later Earl of Devon. Ful-

ton went to work in this region of gloomy but picturesque moors near the English Channel in the . est Country, and the young English aristocrat was pleased with the results. He introduced the still younger American artist into his elite circle of friends, giving Fulton's career as a professional artist the impetus it needed. With the funds received from new commissions, Fulton was able to enjoy a brief respite from his chronic financial problems.

In the last decade of the eighteenth century, Fulton gradually shifted his interest from artistic to mechanical pursuits. This change was partially the result of the influence of several new friends. During his three-year stay in Devonshire, Fulton was to meet two English gentlemen who would have a profound effect on the changing direction of his career—Charles Stanhope, third Earl of Stanhope, and Francis Egerton, third Duke of Bridgewater. Both men had a wide range of interests centered on mechanical devices and transportation schemes. Both were particularly drawn to the idea of propelling boats by steam. It is thought that Fulton met Lord Stanhope first in 1793. The two men often discussed scientific and technical matters, either by mail, or in person.

It is not certain when engineering replaced painting as Fulton's major interest. In the eighteenth century, a mechanical draftsman often had the skills of an artist in order to embellish his engineering drawings. Undoubtedly Fulton was able to easily adapt his artistic ability to mechanical drafting. For a while he dabbled in various endeavors, including developing a marble-sawing device for use in the West Country quarries, a rope-making machine, a modification in the flax spinning wheel, and an improvement in the tanning process for making leather. Although he also seems to have enjoyed speculating on the future of steam transportation, his predominant interest appears to have been canal engineering.

The foremost name in the history of English canals is that of the Duke of Bridgewater, but Fulton's interest in canals was first stimulated by Lord Stanhope, who wanted to construct a canal that would connect the Bristol Channel with the English Channel. In 1796 Fulton wrote, "On perusing a paper descriptive of a canal projected by the Earl of Stanhope, in 1793, where many difficulties seem to arise, my thoughts were first awakened to this subject."[14]

By the fall of 1794 Robert Fulton was living in Manchester in the North Country. He became interested in the Duke of Bridgewater's canal to Liverpool, designed to link Manchester, soon to be industrialized, with the sea. Fulton also met the Duke's very able engineer, James Brindley, and undoubtedly profited from conversations with him.

While at Manchester, Fulton boarded at a dwelling shared by the manufacturer and reformer, Robert Owen, who is probably best known in the United States for the utopian community he established at New Harmony, Indiana, in the 1820s. Fulton was twenty-nine years old and Owen twenty-three when they met. The friendship of the two men grew as they enthusiastically discussed topics of mutual interest, particularly canals. On 17 December 1794, they became partners. Fulton had developed and patented a system of inclined planes that were to employ a winch-like apparatus for hauling canal boats over hilly terrain and was also working on a canal-digging machine. Owen agreed to finance the construction of this latter device, although it is unknown if this machine was ever built. Fulton had heard of a canal project in Gloucester, and in January 1795, he proceeded south to attempt to obtain the construction contract. He described his own machine design as one "for removing earth out of canals to the banks thereof in cases of deep digging without the use of wheelbarrows. . . ."[15] Fulton wrote several letters from Gloucester to his younger Manchester partner. In one of them, using the British slang term for cash, Fulton stated, "When the rhino is gone, I will write to you."[16] By March 1795, the "rhino" had fled, and Fulton, apparently without the contract but still undaunted, returned to Manchester to settle some other outstanding debts, with Owen's help.

Other soon-to-be-famous names graced the Fulton-Owen circle in Manchester. The poet Samuel Taylor Coleridge was a frequent guest. Still in his early twenties, Coleridge visited when he could during his college vacations. Perhaps even more significant for young Fulton was the participation of Dr. John Dalton, the eminent physicist and chemist, in this group. Dalton is now recognized as one of the most important scientists of the modern age. The developer of both the atomic theory and the concept of atomic weight in the early 1800s, he was a key link between Democritus of the ancient world and Einstein of the present century. As a scientist, Dalton may have had some influence on the impressionable young inventor.

Fulton passed the remainder of his residency in England primarily occupied with writing about canals. He returned to London and published a short tract recommending construction of a small canal in the extreme southwestern corner of England in Cornwall for the purpose of hauling coal and agricultural products.

Fulton reached the apex of his work on canals with the publication in 1796 of *A Treatise on the Improvement of Canal Navigation*. Along with *Torpedo War and Submarine Explosions*, written by Fulton in 1810, this book represents one of Fulton's most impressive literary efforts. In fact, the canal treatise is even more ambitious in scope and design than the inventor's later work, illustrated by numerous detailed and skillfully executed drawings of aqueducts, bridges, inclined planes, and other canal appurtenances. Fulton's skill as an artist was serving him well in his nascent engineering career. He began the book with a reference to Lord Stanhope's role in first interesting him in canals, and then, in a brief but fascinating passage, he describes the canal building of the Egyptians, Greeks, Romans, and even a plan by Charlemagne to connect the Rhine and Danube rivers. Fulton refers in his work to Adam Smith, the major proponent of free trade and commerce of the eighteenth century, whose 1776 book, *Inquiry Into the Cause of the Wealth of Nations*, laid the foundation for modern capitalism. Fulton's knowledge of Smith indicates that his later ideas on free trade did not wholly originate during his forthcoming seven-year sojourn in France.[17] In *Canal Navigation*, Fulton envisioned a series of small canals to be used in regions where no alternate feasible transportation system existed. Worldwide in scope, the work also foresaw trains of small, uniform canal boats linked together, much in the fashion of a modern railroad train.

In his canal treatise, Fulton placed great stress on the usage of inclined planes, with which he hoped to replace locks. He wrote: ". . . the first thing that occurred to my imagination, was a water-wheel, to be put in motion by water from the upper level; and by that means, raise the boat on an inclined

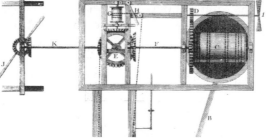

Robert Fulton drawing of inclined plane for his projected canal system. Reprinted from Canal Navigation, *Plate II*

plane. But in great ascents, I found the wheel destroys [i.e. uses] more water than locks. . . ."[18] Fulton also proposed putting wheels on the boats to ease their movement on the plane. His belief in the principle of inclined planes now appears justified by its practical application in the "Main Line" canal route to Pittsburgh in Pennsylvania, completed by mid-nineteenth century. An imaginative combination of locks and an incline railway over the steepest portion of the Appalachian mountains, this Pennsylvania system was started too late to compete successfully with its more famous New York rival the Erie Canal system. Nevertheless, it worked, and the original idea was Fulton's. He wrote in the 1796 treatise, "I will suppose a canal from Philadelphia to Fort-Pit, or any other long line. . . ."[19] Fulton also wrote two letters — one in February and another in March 1796 — to Governor Thomas Mifflin of Pennsylvania, saying that he would like to implement his canal system in his native country. Benjamin West also wrote to the Pennsylvania governor in support of his friend. Mifflin was concerned about inland transportation, but he died in 1799 before anything was done in response to Fulton's initiative. Fulton had recommended state control of the canal, and when the system was finally built years later, the Pennsylvania state government did take control of it, along with other public transportation systems.[20] In the 1820s, the famous Philadelphia pamphleteer, Mathew Carey, sometimes would use the nom de plume "Fulton" while writing in support of Pennsylvania canals.

Robert Fulton sent a copy of his canal treatise to President George Washington, who received it in December 1796, shortly before he was to leave office. While Washington's 14 December reply to Fulton may convey an attitude of polite indifference, on the same day he forwarded Fulton's book to his secretary at Mount Vernon, Tobias Lear, saying, "If the Potomack company can extract anything from it, I shall feel happy in having sent it to you."[21] On 13 January 1799, the "father of his country" wrote a follow-up letter to Lear, expressing concern about the disposition of Fulton's book. No more is heard from George Washington on this subject, and, like Governor Mifflin, he died in 1799.

Fulton made one further American contact of significance during his first ten years in England. William Tatham, a Southerner best known for an essay on the culture of tobacco, had arrived in London in 1796. Tatham met Robert Fulton and they became friends, probably because of a mutual interest in American canal development. They planned to sponsor the construction of a canal from Fayetteville, North Carolina, to Georgetown, South Carolina, which would harness the waters of the major river systems along the way. Nothing came of their scheme, but today at least part of their route is included in the eastern seaboard's intercoastal waterway.

1796 and 1797 were climatic years for Robert Fulton. He had published his canal book and was busily trying to raise money to implement his canal projects. In his search for funds he did not neglect his old friends. He advised Benjamin West, "you will find the time well applied if you devote one day to thoughts on the project."[22] Apparently Fulton wanted the "American Raphael" to put pressure on the Royal Academy for additional backing, as well as to invest his own funds. Fulton also rather frantically asked Lord Stanhope for some aid; presumably he received at least a little relief from his friend.

Fulton had for years depended a great deal upon the financial generosity of Robert Owen. Throughout 1795 and 1796 Fulton periodically told the cotton manufacturer that he regretted his inability to pay him back. Owen's pleasant surprise can be imagined when, in the spring of 1797, he read the following words from Fulton in London:

> . . . having sold one-fourth of my canal prospects for 1500 to a gentleman of large fortune and considerable enterprise, who is gone to reside at New York . . . Now, my friend, this being the state of my money prospects, it becomes necessary that I should deal equal with all my creditors, whose patience in waiting the result of my enterprise I shall long remember with the most heart-felt satisfaction, in which, *thank heaven,* (some men would say *please the pigs,*) I have succeeded . . . I will send 60 as your portion, and pay you the remainder in six months. . . .[23]

Fulton never did pay off his entire debt, but the kindly Owen did not hold that against him. Unfortunately, the identity of Fulton's benefactor has never been discovered, but like the hero Pip of Dicken's work, *Great Expectations*, who one day received a fortune from an unknown source, Fulton's finances were improved from this unidentified partner. Fulton added in the same correspondence, "it is stipulated between my partner and me, that I should go to Paris and obtain patents for the small canal system. . . ."[24] He would leave for the French capital later that year.

Fulton apparently had little sense of the passage of time. He wrote in the 1797 Owen letter: ". . . In about three weeks I mean to set out for Paris, and hope to return in time to be with you at Christmas; and about this time next year I expect to sail for America. . . ."[25] Fulton would not spend another Christmas in England until 1804, and he would not see America until 1806. His first ten years abroad had been important for his artistic training, for developing his skills in canal engineering, and for personal growth. The next ten years in Europe would be momentous ones for Robert Fulton and for naval warfare.

2

The French Connection,
1797–1803

During his seven years residency in France, Robert Fulton would conceive and build an operational submarine. He would also begin his initial experimentation in mine warfare and would formulate a plan to use his steamboat for military troop transport.

On 12 December 1797, roughly six months after he arrived in France, Fulton submitted a comprehensive proposal to the Directory government proposing the construction of a "Mechanical Nautulus [*sic*]" to be used "to annililate" [*sic*] the British navy.[1] With no prior hint of plans or even inclination towards either the invention of a submarine or animosity towards its intended victim, Robert Fulton thus plunged into the field of naval warfare.

The young American had reached Paris in the early summer of 1797, after having been delayed at the Channel port of Calais for three weeks pending official approval of his passport. French relations with America were strained at this time, and the undeclared naval war between France and America known as the Quasi-War was but one year in the future. France had been angered in 1795 by the American ratification of Jay's Treaty, an agreement with England in which the United States failed to insist on its full neutral rights to trade with any nation. Feeling that this agreement represented undue obsequiousness to France's enemy England, the French reacted by

refusing to acknowledge the American minister, C.C. Pinckney, when he arrived in the French capital in December 1796.
Approximately ten months later, in what would become known
as the XYZ Affair, the French government would demand a
large bribe from the three American envoys sent to France to
negotiate a treaty.

Nevertheless, Fulton wrote from Paris in July 1797, "There is
every symptom of my remaining here in peace, although the
Americans are by no means well received or suffered to rest in
quiet."[2] Fulton, ever the optimist, put all unpleasant thoughts
behind him as he began his new adventure. Seeing everything
in Paris as "gay and joyous," the thirty-one-year-old American
rather immodestly stated, "I have good reason to believe there
will be good encouragement to men of genius."[3]

As will be recalled, Robert Fulton had come to France in
order to procure a patent for his canal project. He spent much
of his time during the initial weeks in Paris drawing up sketches
and drafts for that document. Government officials found no
problems with his application, and on 14 February 1798, he
was awarded a patent on his canal system, effective for fifteen
years. Fulton was pleased. He wrote to Earl Stanhope, "Since
my arrival in Paris, I have been active in my Canal pursuits,
And on this subject I have Created a Revolution In the mind of
all the French engeneers [sic] I have met with."[4]

Fulton also forwarded a copy of his canal treatise to Napoleon Bonaparte. Bonaparte's coup d'etat of 18 Brumaire (the
French date for 9 November 1799) was almost two years in the
future. In the spring of 1798 he was about to embark on his
military and scientific expedition to Egypt. As one can imagine, he had little time for thoughts of a world made more
peaceful and prosperous by a vast canal network. Fulton may
have realized this. In November 1798, he wrote to Joshua Gilpin, an American businessman then living in Europe, "For the
pleasure of seeing my Canal system stand in its true Light I
look to America, as to America I look for the perfectioning of
all my plans."[5]

Shortly after arriving in Paris, Fulton met the man who was
to be the greatest single influence on his life, work, and

thought, the American writer and statesman, Joel Barlow. Through his monetary and political aid, his school and family connections, his constant friendship and encouragement, as well as the similarity of his ideas to the young inventor's, Barlow was to play an extremely important role in the story of Robert Fulton and naval warfare.

While most accounts indicate that Joel Barlow was born in Redding, Connecticut, on 24 March 1754, the birth date his widow inscribed on a commemorative tablet in Poland was 1756. This would make him at least nine years older than Robert Fulton. Like the younger American, there is little data on Barlow's youth that can be corroborated. As did Fulton, he spent some of his early life on a farm. He attended Dartmouth in 1772 and transferred to Yale two years later. When the Revolution broke out, he volunteered for military service and participated in the debacle of the Battle of Long Island in 1776. This experience brought the fighting phase of his military career to a close, and he returned to Yale, where he was designated class poet. He graduated in 1778 and then taught school in New Haven for a time, but without enthusiasm. Rather desperately, Barlow searched for a profession. Apparently without either the proper spiritual or secular motivation, he obtained a position as army chaplain with a Massachusetts brigade. Developing his interests in poetry, Barlow used his leisure time in diverse army camps to work on his first major poem, *Vision of Columbus*. After the war, he started a weekly newspaper in Hartford and dabbled in book publishing. Ever the diversified young American, he read law and was admitted to the Connecticut bar in 1786. His writing continued and in this year he contributed to a multi-authored poem, *The Anarchiad*, which castigated rebellions of the type led by Daniel Shays. Barlow's contribution to this poem connected him with a group of poets of the time known as the Connecticut Wits. These writers used sarcasm to mock the "anarchy" they saw in state governments and the Articles of Confederation and pushed for a stronger central government similar to the one soon to be set up by the Constitution.

Sometime in the next two years, Barlow embarked on the most criticized episode of his life, one that would bring him directly to Paris and ultimately to his encounter with Fulton in 1797. Barlow, along with other former members of the revolutionary army, joined former revolutionary leader Manasseh Cutler, William Duer and others in a grandiose scheme of speculation in lands along the banks of the Ohio River. Huge profits for all were supposedly to result from the sale of this land. There was only one slight drawback in the scheme of

Joel Barlow, painted by Robert Fulton, 1805. Indianapolis Museum of Art, Gift of Mr. and Mrs. Eli Lilly, Sr.

which Barlow was not aware: Duer and his partners, who called themselves the "Scioto Associates," did not own the land they planned to sell. Because of the international fame Barlow had achieved with his poem on Columbus, Cutler proposed to send him to Europe to find buyers for the western lands. Duer agreed. Barlow accepted, and in 1788 arrived in France prepared to do business. He became partners with a rather devious English promoter with the deliciously ironic name of William Playfair, and the two men described to the French an impressive city-to-be in the wilderness called Gallipolis, or "City of the French." Playfair became so carried away with his own rhetoric that he indicated that the American national capital would soon be moved there! Thousands of French citizens subscribed to the planned colony and Barlow notified Duer in 1790 that hundreds of French colonists would soon be sailing for this new paradise. Duer was shattered. He frantically contracted to buy some land, for which he never paid, from the neighboring Ohio Company. The emigrants ultimately arrived at "Gallipolis" on the north bank of the Ohio, near the mouth of the Kanawha River. As Duer never had bought any land, the colony was a miserable failure, and much of the angry French reaction was directed at Barlow. This period in the early 1790's was the nadir of his life.

Barlow recovered from his Gallipolis misadventure after the publication of his most important prose work, *Advice to the Privileged Orders in the Several States of Europe*, in 1792. *Advice to the Privileged Orders*, along with Thomas Paine's *Rights of Man* (1791–1792), was a reaction against Edmund Burke's influential primer against uprising entitled *Reflections on the Revolution in France* (1790). Up to this time, Barlow's association with the Connecticut Wits had earned him a reputation as a political conservative. His friendship with Paine and English liberals, however, plus additional considerations such as his dislike for Burke's style, moved Barlow permanently into the liberal camp from 1791 on. Referring to one of Burke's speeches, Barlow once said, "He rises like a rocket, spreads a glaring light, and comes down like a stick!"[6] In *Advice to the Privileged Orders*, Barlow idealistically visualized an economically abundant democracy free from class privilege, in which science and reason would be used as the primary means to solve society's problems. Robert Fulton would find himself in complete agreement with these principles.

Barlow's new prose writings dispersed most of the bitter reaction to his Gallipolis venture. He was made a citizen of France in 1793 and wrote his best poem, *The Hasty Pudding*, that year in Savoy. He also supported himself quite well during this period by providing the French with war supplies in their struggle against the First Coalition, a group of major European powers which had united in 1793 against France. From early 1796 to late 1797, he served as U.S. consul to Algiers and arranged treaties with Tunis, Algiers, and Tripoli. He returned to Paris in September of that year, preparing to return finally to America. What kept Barlow in France for another eight years is not certain, but it was at this juncture that he first met Fulton.

When he first arrived in Paris, Fulton took a room at the same hotel in which Barlow and his wife had been living since Barlow's recent return from North Africa. The three people met, and the Barlows were immediately attracted to the handsome and charming younger American. The nature and the diversity of the ideas they discussed as well as their similarities in experiences undoubtedly strengthened the relationship. Fulton was roughly ten years younger than the childless couple, and he began to be seen more and more frequently in their company, gradually assuming the role of a combination younger brother and son. When the Barlows asked him to move in with them, he readily accepted.

The Barlows had been married secretly in 1781 and during their life together were an impressively affectionate couple. One letter in particular, written by the lonely husband in Algiers to his wife in France, illustrates this point:

> Dear idol of my heart, twenty-nine of your charming letters were thrown onto my bed the other day before I had gotten up. Ah, if only they were their dear author. . . . I love you, my angel. No, you are not an angel. One cannot love an angel, an imaginary being, as I love you. You are my flesh and my blood, my life, my soul and my spirit, you are my

delight, my food, my hope for the future, my actual joy. And you ask me if I love you! When I find myself in your arms again I will tell you if I love you![7]

Robert Fulton became exceedingly close to Ruth Barlow, whom he nicknamed "Ruthinda." He proved an excellent companion for her when her husband was away on frequent business trips, and often escorted her to the various French spas she frequented because of her generally poor health. Mrs. Barlow became upset whenever Fulton indicated he was interested enough in a girl to consider marrying her. She scotched a budding interest in an English woman and was very upset when Fulton finally did marry the American Harriet Livingston in 1807; "Ruthinda" avoided the Fultons for months. While a modern and more cynical age might view Ruth's relations with Fulton and especially their long trips alone together with titilated disapproval, Joel Barlow was so certain — and correctly so — of both his wife's love and of his young friend's goodwill that he could laugh at the situation. Once, when he was returning from a trip to England, Barlow conjured up the following imaginary dialogue between his wife and Fulton together back in Paris:

Wife — Ah, where's my dear Hubby, Whom Fate, in its malice Snatched away long ago.
Toot — Now, I'll bet he's at Calais.
Wife — I'll bet he's not, though. But, Tooty, my dear, Suppose him at Calais, when think he'll be here?
Toot — Be here! Let us count. This is Thursday you say, His passport and baggage will take the whole day; Then other vexations fall in by the hundred — Surrounded, examined, palavered, and plundered. But he'll set off to-morrow, and then, I divine, We shall have him next Sunday between us to dine; For he'll whirl along rapidly through the relays, Cheek by jowl with Machere, and in Parker's post-chaise.
Wife — All that's but a fancy. I'll bet what you dare He's not here on Sunday, nor is he now there.
Toot — I'll hold you ten guineas, and sixpence to boot.
Wife — Done.

Toot—Done, here's my hand for't.
Hub. —I'll go halves with Toot.[8]

"Toot" is, of course, Robert Fulton, a nickname given to him
by the Barlows. The origin of the nickname is not known, and
only a real stretch of the imagination could connect it with the
whistle of a steamboat at this time.

In addition to being Fulton's best friend, Joel Barlow was
also his teacher. In the classroom of their new home, the elder,
more cosmopolitan American coached the younger Fulton for
hours on end in French, German, and Italian, as well as in
other scientific and philosophical subjects. Barlow, in turn,
became infected with Fulton's excitement over canals, and
wrote a letter addressed "To the Citizens of the United States,"
which called for Americans to adopt, among other things·
". . . A system of small canals, as projected by one of our most
estimable citizens, on a plan so extensive as to take place generally of public roads in the most frequented routes. . . . it
would greatly serve to harmonize the interests of the states, and
to strengthen their present union."[9] Barlow acknowledged that
Fulton had inspired his belated interest in a canal system in the
introduction to his half-completed poem called "The Canal":

Yes, my dear FULTON, let us seize the lyre,
and give to science all the Muse's fire,
Mount on the boat, and as it glides along,
We'll cheer the long Canal with useful song.[10]

Joel Barlow's affections for the younger American had no
limits. During one of the many joint absences of his wife and
Fulton, Barlow wrote Ruth, "I am glad to hear of Toot's success in experiment. Always repeat to him how much I love him;
you cannot tell him too much of it. I shall send him some
money tomorrow."[11] Once Robert Fulton had determined to
build a submarine of his own, Joel Barlow encouraged him and
helped him to finance it.

Barlow probably paid his highest compliment to Robert Fulton when he dedicated the revised "Columbus" poem, now
called *Columbiad*, to him. Years later, Fulton drew twelve il-

lustrations for the 1807 edition, which would gain the reputation of being the most beautiful and expensive book produced up to that time in the United States. Barlow wrote the following words to Fulton in that edition, "My dear friend—This poem is your property. . . . Take it then to yourself and let it live a monument to our friendship."[12]

There should be no question now as to the close relationship of Joel Barlow and Robert Fulton. It is my belief that they also shared similar ideas on naval warfare. While there is no direct evidence, the record suggests that Joel Barlow's philosophical ideas on the military and warfare may have stimulated, at least in part, Fulton's new but absorbing interest in the field. It is difficult to determine who inspired whom on this particular subject, but most probably their ideas were nearly equipollent. Barlow's *Advice to the Privileged Orders* might reasonably be assumed to have served as the starting point for the two friends' interchange of ideas.

In this book Barlow's attack on class privilege called for the elimination of standing armies. In addition to removing the apparatus of war, this action would also, in Barlow's opinion, remove the military buttressing of the aristocracy and stimulate the masses' interest in self-government. Barlow did not mention specifically naval warfare, but his general military concepts would serve as the foundation for later writings by Robert Fulton. The younger American made no direct reference to the military of note before arriving in France, but in his 1796 *A Treatise on the Improvement of Canal Navigation* he did indicate in very general terms his burgeoning interest in labor, commerce, and free trade.

Once in France, however, Robert Fulton's thoughts on commerce soon became imbued with Barlow's antipathy towards the military. In a long paper on free trade entitled, "To the Friends of Mankind," Fulton attacked warfare in general, concomitantly praising free trade. One phrase in this paper, "Industry will give abundance to a virtuous world," so caught men's imaginations that it was conveyed by carrier pigeons in the joint commemorative celebration in 1909 of Fulton's 1807 Hudson River steamboat and Henry Hudson's discovery of that river in 1609.[13] In the fall of 1797, Fulton went much further. He specifically attacked the role of navies in a long treatise entitled "Thoughts on Free Trade," which he submitted to the Directory on 9 October. Setting forth in this document the theme that "foreign possessions and all duties on *importation is injurious to Nations,*" Fulton said that if free trade were to be established among the major nations, the threat of war would largely be removed. The inventor then turned to the navy by noting, "France cannot think of keeping up a fleet sufficient to prevent the trade of England with other nations. . . ." Developing this idea, he concluded that, once free trade is established: ". . . Navies with all their complications of Admiralties, Naval Stores, Press Gangs and infinite horrors, which imbetter [sic] the Life of Men and disgrace Common Sense will then be done away."[14]

"Thoughts on Free Trade" is much closer to Robert Fulton's December 1797 naval proposal to the Directory than the other Fulton and Barlow sources cited. Is there a plausible explanation for Fulton's new emphasis on navies? Much of the credit for originality must be given to Fulton himself, in the absence of direct evidence to the contrary. However, it is just possible that someone else may have directed Fulton's thoughts towards the Navy. Fulton may have unwittingly left a clue as to the identity of this person in the last sentence quoted above from "Thoughts on Free Trade" by his reference to "Common Sense."

Thomas Paine's *Rights of Man*, which he published in London the same year Barlow produced *Advice to the Privileged Orders*, was also an angry reaction to Burke's commentary on the French Revolution. Paine's book, along with his previous tract *Common Sense*, has had, of course, a greater effect on revolutionary movements than Barlow's work. Barlow was himself much taken with it, and he and Paine became good friends after meeting in London during one of Barlow's trips to England. In *Rights of Man*, Paine carried Barlow's general criticism of the military a step further by specifically condemning navies as impediments to commerce among nations. Paine proposed cutting back all naval forces to ten percent of their existing sizes. This action, he hypothesized, would bring about both vast monetary savings and a more lasting peace for all nations.[15] Paine soon left England forever for France, and after Robert Fulton arrived there, Barlow's friendship for both men brought them together. The three often met and dined in Paris, and while Paine and Fulton's relationship largely centered around their mutual interest in the engineering of iron bridges and steamboats, Paine was also curious about Fulton's developing naval ideas. Years later, after both men had returned to America, Paine wrote to Barlow, "What is Fulton about? Is he taming a whale to draw his submarine boat?"[16] Even if Paine did not relate directly to Fulton his plan to reduce navies by ten percent, it is likely that Barlow did in the course of their many hours of philosophical discussion.

The question of the submarine can now be raised. Why was this particular vessel selected, and where did Fulton get the idea? In an 1806 tract entitled "Motives for Inventing Submarine Navigation and Attack," Fulton observed that, after having considered the problem of reducing navies for several months, he came to see that he could accomplish this with two inventions — an underwater boat and an underwater explosive device.[17] He did not explain further, but most scholars believe that Fulton used many of the concepts of his American predecessor in this field, David Bushnell. Ironically, a good case has recently been made that Bushnell derived most of his underwater warfare ideas from the French inventor of the late 1600s, Denis Papin, who in turn gained much of his inspiration from the Dutch inventor of the early 1600s, Cornelius Drebbel, and others.[18]

Like Barlow, David Bushnell had been born in Connecticut, but some years earlier. Bushnell began experimenting with underwater warfare during his first year at Yale. During the early years of the American Revolution he built a one-man submarine which he called the *Turtle*. With dimensions of seven and one-half feet by six feet, it was quite small and hardly resembled the cigar-like shape of the modern submarine. The *Turtle* floated, bobbing, just below the surface, with only its small, primitive conning tower exposed. The boat was propelled

manually, the operator steering with his right hand at the same
time turning with his left hand a crank that turned the propeller. The operator could also submerge the *Turtle* by letting
water into a bottom tank and raise it by expelling the water
with a foot pump. In 1776 Bushnell planned to attack Admiral
Richard Howe's flagship in New York harbor. Sergeant Ezra
Lee was chosen and trained to guide the *Turtle* to its target.
The craft was to make its approach on the surface, and then
submerge as it closed in. Lee was to maneuver the *Turtle*
under the large warship and then manually drill an auger into
its bottom. A line would have an explosive charge attached to
one end; the other end would be run through an eye on the
auger. As the *Turtle* moved away from the ship, the explosive
charge would then be pulled into contact with the target ship.
This would actuate a time-lock mechanism, which would be set
to allow the *Turtle*'s operator time to withdraw from the
target. The mission did not succeed, apparently because of the
complexity of the mechanical operations, the lack of control
underwater, and the toughness of the target hull. However, the
1776 *Turtle* mission should not be regarded as a complete
failure. For the first time in history, a man made an underwater attack in a submarine, and, although he did not sink the
target ship, he maneuvered his own craft beneath it, and then
was able to withdraw successfully. The following year Bushnell
conducted a floating mine operation on the Delaware River.
After engaging in a variety of enterprises, none really success-

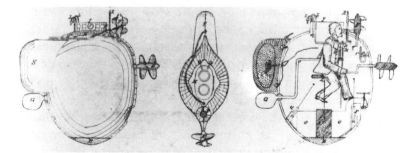

1885 drawing of David Bushnell's American Turtle, *1776. Smithsonian Institution*

ful, he apparently went to Europe in the 1780s and returned to the United States in 1795. He died in 1826.

Scholarly opinion does not agree as to whether Robert Fulton and David Bushnell did, in fact, meet in Europe and discuss the submarine: There is no direct evidence to support such a meeting, but this does not mean absolutely that it did not occur.[19] For one thing, Fulton may have had the opportunity to meet Bushnell during a short visit he made to France in 1790. Also, a statement made in the memoirs of Duchess de Gontaut, a French aristocrat with whom Fulton had a brief encounter while waiting for passport approval in Calais during the summer of 1797, implies that such a meeting could have occurred. Fulton had met this femme fatale aboard the channel boat crossing from England to France when he appealed to her for help in translating a French directive. The duchess was traveling incognito, attempting to pass herself off as a nondescript citizen. Upon landing, both Fulton and the duchess were detained for three weeks by French officials, and Fulton learned that his mysterious new friend was suspected of being an important aristocrat. (Dickens again seems appropriate, this time *A Tale of Two Cities,* which describes the problems of aristocrats secretly trying to return to France during the revolution.) Fulton now made the most impulsive and romantic gesture of his life up to this time. In an effort to save the lady, he gallantly offered to marry her! She thanked him, but told him she was already married, and ultimately extricated herself from the unpleasantness with the government. She and Fulton parted company, but they would meet again. Now this would be just a pleasant and humanizing anecdote were it not that the Duchess later alleged that Fulton had made the following significant comment when she turned down his offer to save her: "Oh, what a pity, what a pity! I would make you rich, I am going to make my fortune in Paris. I have invented a steamboat, and I am going to set the whole world going. Besides, I have invented a way of blowing up an enemy's fleet by means of submarine boats; nothing could be easier."[20] Now the question is this: If Fulton made such a statement regarding "submarine boats" in the summer of 1797, where did he get the idea? As there is no evidence of any other source up to this point, the duchess's statement does support the hypothesis of a possible meeting with Bushnell in 1790. However, the duchess also referred to Fulton having already "invented a steamboat" in 1797 and Fulton did not have an operational steamboat until 1803. It is more probable that the duchess remembered incorrectly as she was reconstructing the events of 1797 in her mind several years later, following Fulton's fame in America.

On the other hand, a case can be made that Fulton learned of Bushnell's ideas from his good friend, Joel Barlow. Barlow was a freshman at Yale when Bushnell was a senior there and deeply involved in his submarine experiments. Even more significantly, Barlow's brother-in-law and former roommate, Abraham Baldwin, was a close friend of Bushnell's and helped him get re-established back in the United States. It is probably more likely that Barlow and Bushnell conversed in France on submarine warfare and that Barlow passed Bushnell's key comments on to Fulton, than it is that Bushnell met Fulton in Europe sometime before Bushnell's departure in 1795, two years preceding Fulton's move to France.

Let the reader now return to Robert Fulton's formal proposal of 12 December 1797 to the French Directory government on naval warfare, which began by calling attention to the power of the English navy. He wished to build the "Mechanical Nautulus" in order to destroy that fleet. Fulton then told the French government that he had already found financial backers, with whom he had formed the "Nautulus Company." This company would be responsible for building and operating the submarine, provided that the government pay for each English ship destroyed by Fulton's invention. Fulton also proposed that all prizes become the property of the company, that the Directory allow him the right to dispatch his submarine from any French port, and that, to preclude execution for piracy, the crew be given commissions stating that violation of their rights as prisoners-of-war would result in French retaliation on English prisoners "au quadruple," meaning that for every one of Fulton's crew harmed, the French would punish four English prisoners.[21]

One significant condition of Fulton's proposal was that the invention not be used by the French against the United States. While Robert Fulton's naval dealings with France and England were at the very least questionable, his loyalty towards the United States was always steadfast. He concluded his proposal with a hope that the French would signify their support as quickly as possible in order to better secure "la Liberte des mers."

While Fulton never specifically identified the nature of his invention in this proposal, he did refer to "toute expedition sous-marine."[22] This phrase, along with the fish-like name of his invention, are sufficient clues to its identity. The word "nautilus" — Fulton soon corrected the spelling — refers to an ocean mollusk having a shell of air-filled chambers. Although Jules Verne's fictional submarine, the *Nautilus,* of *Twenty-Thousand Leagues Under the Sea* and Admiral Rickover's atomic-powered submarine, also the *Nautilus*, might be better known, Robert Fulton was the first person to give a submarine this name.

Three months before Robert Fulton submitted his submarine proposal, the five-man Directory had experienced the coup d'etat of 18 Fructidor (4 September 1797) which removed one of its members, Nicolas Carnot, who might possibly have been sympathetic to Fulton's project. Most of the remaining directors appear to have been hard-working and solid, if unimaginative, men. Fulton corresponded with Citizen Director La Revelliere-Lepeaux at this time, but to no avail. The Directory forwarded Fulton's proposal to the Minister of Marine for examination and recommendation. The chief naval minister was Georges Rene Pleville-le-Pelley, a seventy-one-year-old admiral who had participated in the d'Estaing campaign during the American Revolution in 1778.[23] Pleville-le-Pelley accepted some of Fulton's proposals; however, he wanted Fulton's fee for each British gun destroyed cut in half, and he refused to grant commissions of safety to the submarine crew. Fulton agreed to the monetary cut, but he persisted with his demand for protective documents for his crew. The negotiations broke down on this issue, and on 5 February 1798, Fulton was advised that his project had been rejected. Pleville-le-Pelley indicated that not only would Fulton's weapon not be operating in accordance with the traditional rules of war, but also his proposal for punishment "au quadruple " would be an ineffective threat as the British had more prisoners than the French upon whom to heap reprisals. So ended the first phase of Fulton's French negotiations.[24]

Despite this unfavorable response from the government, Robert Fulton continued to promote his project. He elicited an inspection from a team of distinguished French scientists, including mathematician Gaspard Monge and the famed balloonist Montgolfier. Fulton was acquainted with both men. On 16 February 1798, he wrote to his English inventor friend Edmund Cartwright: " . . . The celebrated Montgolfier has just made a great discovery in hydraulics; it is a means of raising water from the beds of rivers by the simple movement of the stream. . . . I know him well, and have seen his model frequently at work."[25]

Fulton hoped that Admiral Eustache Bruix, who had been named Minister of Marine and was much younger than Pleville-le-Pelley might be more receptive to new ideas. On 23 July 1798, Fulton again requested consideration of his submarine project. His hunch regarding the young admiral's sympathy initially seemed justified, for Bruix reopened negotiations by convening a commission of scientists to examine and report on Fulton's progress. Among the commissioners was Citizen Adet, a unique combination of scientist and politician. As evidenced by his 1789 tract on curing ulcers, Adet, who was a chemist, sometimes extended his work into the field of medicine. He also sometimes exceeded his authority as his government's representative; for example, earlier in the 1790s he had become deeply involved in domestic partisan politics in the United States with his newspaper attacks on George Washington's Federalist administration. Bruix's appointment letter to Adet indicates that all of the commissioners were directed to meet at Fulton's Parisian residence at eleven o'clock in the morning on 2 August to examine his project.[26]

The seven French commissioners accordingly met, consid-

ered what they saw and heard, and duly submitted an extensive report to Bruix on 5 September 1798. They described Fulton's submarine plans in detail and enthusiastically supported
them. While the fact that most of these men were respected scientists was important for Fulton, it was also significant that two
of the seven men, Adet and another, were politically oriented.
Adet's near-frantic republicanism may have made him more
sympathetic to Fulton, whose own political ideals were developing along similar lines.

Joel Barlow was, of course, an ardent republican, and, as
evidenced by some events of that summer, his close association
with Fulton may have earned for the inventor a similar reputation. In August, George Logan, an American Quaker, had
come to France as a private citizen actively attempting to improve the diplomatic climate between France and the United
States. Barlow and Fulton received him enthusiastically and escorted him around Paris. One social high point of Logan's
three-week sojourn was a dinner party at the English writer
Helen Marie Williams's salon in company with Barlow and
Fulton. Other than serving as inspiration for the passage of the
Logan Act (January 1799), which forbids unauthorized diplo-
macy by private citizens, Logan really did not accomplish very
much.

The American government at this time was Federalist, and
adamantly opposed to the views of the Republicans. William
Vans Murray, the Federalist diplomat officially trying to end
the Quasi-War with France, raged at both Logan and Barlow
for their meddling. Murray's attitude towards Fulton is not
known, but it is logical to assume that he classified him along
with Logan and that "puffing toad" Barlow as being Republicans disloyal to the Federalist government for having acted
without its authority. Fulton worried about this type of cate-
gorization. In November 1798 he wrote:

> From what I have heard, Some of my friends fear that I may
> become an instrument in the hands of party—but of this I
> believe there is not the least danger. If I know myself I
> believe I am much governed by my own Comtemplations

which Comtemplations I believe always tend to promote the Interests of Mankind — at least Such is my wish. . . . [27]

Fulton's friend and first biographer Colden observed of him, "He was decidedly a republican. . . . but his zeal for his opinions or party, did not extinguish his kindness for the merits of his opponents."[28]

The greatest significance of the 5 September 1798 commissioners' report was that it described for the first time Robert Fulton's submarine designs. The description is extensive, and, as it has been quoted in full in other works, will just be briefly summarized in this study.[29] Although Fulton had not yet constructed his submarine, and was then just at the drawing stage, he had been very thorough in his proposals and specifications. Much of his design appeared to be related to Bushnell's craft, but there were some major differences. For one thing, despite the commissioners' description of the boat as ellipsoidal,

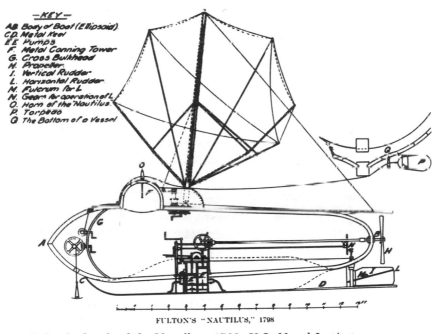

FULTON'S "NAUTILUS," 1798

Fulton's sketch of the Nautilus, *1798. U.S. Naval Institute*

Fulton's drawing shows a boat that was much more elongated than the *Turtle*. In fact, Fulton's *Nautilus* was the first definitely cigar-shaped submarine. Fulton also proposed to use hand cranks instead of Bushnell's foot pedal to turn the screw propeller in order to better control the submarine's vertical movement. Finally, whereas Bushnell built a small craft able to carry just one man, Fulton envisioned a vessel capable of holding several men. When the *Nautilus* was actually completed and tested in 1801, it proved to be much more seaworthy and more stable when submerging than Bushnell's *Turtle*, which had bobbed clumsily in New York harbor in 1776. One passage of the commissioners' report deserves to be quoted; in fact, the French naval authority at the turn of the twentieth century, Maurice Delpeuch, used it in 1907 to dedicate a book he had written on submarines. He quoted the commissioners as saying: "The weapon conceived by Citizen Fulton is a means of terrible destruction, because it acts in silence and in an almost inevitable manner. It is particularly suited to the French, because having (one should necessarily say) a feebler navy than its adversary, the entire destruction of both is advantageous for them."[30] This statement reflected the heart of Robert Fulton's own views on naval warfare which were that his weapon could be used to destroy all navies and thus end war, and had implications above and beyond the French wars of this particular period. While noting imperfections in the design of the craft, the commissioners summed up their feelings by saying, "It is the first conception of a man of genius."[31] They concluded by recommending approval of the project and that tests be conducted.

This report must have made the American inventor feel secure about the acceptance of his project, because on 18 October, he amended his proposals to include a reward of 500,000 francs after the first English ship was destroyed. Planning to use this money to build a fleet of submarines, Fulton also requested additional rewards for each calibre gun destroyed. Admiral Bruix's response to either the commissioners' report or to Fulton's new demands is not known. As the weeks passed with no word, Fulton must have become increasingly nervous. On

27 October 1798, he went over the admiral's head to write to Director Paul Barras. This move is somewhat surprising, as Barras is generally regarded by historians as one of the least savory of French leaders in this period; Fulton's move must reflect his desperation. Fulton advised Citizen Director Barras of the commissioners' report, and described what he envisioned to be the weapon's potential effect on England. Fulton noted that British commerce depended on the Royal Navy and then wrote:

> . . . warships destroyed by means so new, so secret, and so incalculable, the confidence of the sailors is destroyed, and the fleet rendered worthless in the age of the Jeremiahs of fright. In this state of things, the English republicans will rise to facilitate the descent of the French, to change their government themselves, without shedding much blood, and with any cost to France.[32]

Fulton concluded his letter by forecasting that the successful English revolutionaries would then practice freedom of the seas, which in turn would guarantee perpetual peace. This would mitigate any alleged inhumanity associated with his weapon. Fulton was increasingly concerned with the public's negative reaction to the silent nature of his submarine. The English first heard of his concept in August 1798, when one of Fulton's American friends in Europe, Joshua Gilpin, told Fulton's old companion, Lord Stanhope, of Fulton's submarine negotiations then underway in France. Fulton expressed his concern over the English public's antipathy to his invention in a letter to Gilpin on 20 November:

> . . . The plan of my Nautilus you say is not liked. This must be because its Consequences are not understood. The idea is yet an infant but I think I see in it all the nerve and muscle of an Infant hercules which at one grasp will Strangle the Serpents which poison and Convulse the American Constitution. . . . [33]

Fulton believed that his submarine would remove the English and French threat to the United States by destroying their navies. Although he had not seen America for more than ten years, Fulton's letter of 20 November is further evidence of his constant loyalty to the United States. This same correspondence also shows that Fulton increasingly associated his naval warfare concepts with the United States. On the very day in 1798 that the French captured the American schooner *Retaliation*, and the Quasi-War began, Fulton continued in his letter to Gilpin:

> . . . a perfect free trade is of the utmost importance particularly to America. I would ask any one if all the American difficulties during this war is not owing to the Naval Systems of Europe and a Liscensed Robery [*sic*] on the Ocean? How then is America to prevent this? Certainly not by attempting to build a fleet to cope with the fleets of Europe, but if possible by Rendering the European fleets useless.[34]

Like Bruix, Barras did not respond to Fulton's new appeal. Following this second failure to interest the French in his ideas on naval warfare, Robert Fulton pursued a variety of other interests. Although some accounts indicate that he may have gone to Holland at this time to promote his submarine, there is no solid evidence to support this. He did make a model of a rope-making machine at this time, but graciously told his friend, industrialist Edmund Cartwright, that the Englishman's design was better. He also continued painting, completing at least two oils of Joel Barlow and one of Barlow's wife Ruth. Fulton's most significant non-nautical activity, and the one that made him the most money, was the conception of a huge panorama which he painted in Paris. The first such panorama, a display of large pictures of epic historical subjects, was developed by Robert Barker in Britain a few years earlier. Fulton is said to have seen Barker's work and witnessed the ensuing large profits. In association with an American named James Thayer, Fulton took out a French patent for a panorama in 1799. A building site was selected along the Boulevard Montmartre which is still known as *Passage des Panoramas*; a nearby street was also named after Fulton. The historical picture that Fulton painted was called "The Burning of Moscow."

While the subject was not, of course, Napoleon's defeat in Russia a dozen years in the future, the theme was both ironically and sadly prescient. Fulton was soon to have a frustrating association with Napoleon regarding his naval warfare inventions, and Fulton's best friend, Barlow, was to die accompanying Napoleon on the 1812 Moscow campaign. Fulton's panorama was popular in France, and the idea was extremely well received in America. His work is believed to have served as the inspiration for the later American panoramas of his friend, Rembrandt Peale, as well as those of John Vanderlyn and others.[35]

During this period, a young Frenchman named Eleuthere Irenee Du Pont asked Fulton for advice on opportunities in the United States. Although Fulton's glowing description of America largely centered on the country's agricultural potential, it must have been effective. Du Pont arrived in the United States in 1800 and soon founded his famous powder plant at Wilmington, Delaware.

In a letter written on 3 July 1799 to his mother, Fulton indicated that he was so busy at the time that he had not even had time to fall in love. He admitted, however, that this was partially because he wanted someday to marry some nice American girl. A reference in his letter to his being an old bachelor of thirty-two is perhaps an indication of how engrossed he was in his diverse interests; at this time, Fulton was just four months shy of being thirty-four years old.[36]

On 17 July 1799, Admiral Bruix was replaced as minister of Marine, and Fulton attempted to reopen negotiations with his successor, Bourbon de Vatry, but to no avail. In a letter to de Vatry on 5 October, Fulton stressed the morality of his new invention, again calling for official support, and complained of certain French naval officers who were not friendly to the *Nautilus*.

Suddenly, as a result of Napoleon Bonaparte's coup d'etat of 18 Brumaire (9 November 1799), Robert Fulton's efforts on behalf of his submarine received new support. One of the several subsequent changes made in personnel was the replacement of de Vatry as minister of Marine by P. A. L. Forfait. Forfait was not only a very well known naval designer, but he also had been one of the members of the favorably disposed commission that examined Fulton's submarine design in 1798. His appointment was a fortunate one for Fulton, for Forfait was to become, for a time, the foremost official champion of Fulton's naval experiments.

Up to this time, Fulton's work on the submarine had been largely confined to the drawing board. There is no solid primary evidence to support an allegation made by some that Fulton and Barlow had conducted experiments on some crude type of propelled torpedo on the Seine River, and had almost been killed in the process.[37] Now, with Napoleon and Forfait in power, Fulton finally began to construct the *Nautilus*. The vessel was built at the Perrier workshop located by the Seine. The boat was made out of copper and was sometimes called

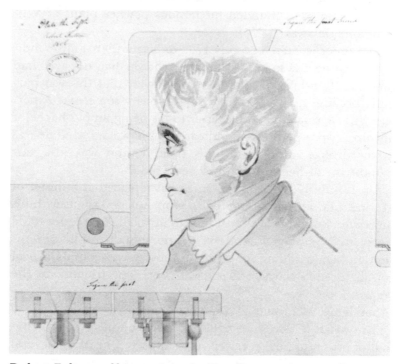

Robert Fulton, self-portrait in the Nautilus *conning tower, 1806. Alofsen Collection, The New Jersey Historical Society, Alan Frazer, photographer*

"Batteau Poisson," indicating both boat and fish. In April 1800, Fulton advised Forfait that the boat was almost completed and submitted anew proposals stressing the need for protective commissions for the crew. The records are silent as to whether any official decision was made at this time. Nevertheless, Fulton continued putting the final touches on this initial assemblage of the *Nautilus*.

Contrary to some older accounts which stated that the submarine was built and completed at Rouen in July 1800, Fulton's *Nautilus* was built and first tested on the Seine at Paris on 13 June of that year. Forfait observed this test personally and told Napoleon that it was very successful. He remarked that the boat submerged easily, remained under water for forty-five minutes, and that the three-man crew apparently suffered no ill effects. The crew consisted of Fulton, an American named Nathaniel Sergeant, and a Frenchman named Fleuret. Forfait also noted that in order to ensure sufficient oxygen for the crew and to keep the candles lit, which were the sole means of illumination, jars of oxygen neutralized with lime were used to supplement the air supply. The submarine was also tested on the surface under sail. Forfait advised the First Consul that Fulton had already spent 28,000 francs on his invention and was now asking the government for only 6,000 additional francs. The minister implied that Fulton was still requesting protective commissions; however, Forfait advised his superior that other means could be found to placate Fulton on this matter. Only one technical problem was noted, and that was not the fault of the inventor. The Seine at Paris was not deep enough to effectively test the ability of the submarine to withstand underwater depth pressure, and the current was too strong to conclusively test the maneuverability of the vessel. Consequently, further tests were planned downstream at Rouen where the river was broader and deeper. Forfait ended his report by stating that he felt these experiments were so important that he wanted permission to go to Rouen incognito and continue his observations from there.[38]

Fulton also wrote to Napoleon about this first experiment with the submarine. The American inventor stressed his favorite theme of destroying English maritime power and thus establishing freedom of the seas. He also reiterated his desire for protective commissions, as he greatly feared the English would treat the submarine crew as pirates if captured, due to the nature of the vessel. Fulton enclosed a form letter for Napoleon's approval and signature. This letter stated that, if Fulton and his crew were taken by the English and were not treated as prisoners-of-war, Napoleon would use "de droit de talion" (the right of retaliation) on captured English officers and seamen.[39]

Napoleon did not respond personally to Fulton's letter, and, early in September, Forfait advised Joel Barlow that it would not be possible to obtain the protective commissions that Fulton so ardently desired. Then, unexplainedly, the next day Forfait's aide told Barlow that the requested commissions had been approved and dispatched. It is not clear, however, whether or not Fulton actually did receive them. The only description known of the alleged commissions is in a letter written on 12 October 1800 in Paris by a New England sea captain named Israel Thrask. Thrask wrote that Fulton "has the grade of an Admiral from this government," and that Fulton's two companions had been commissioned as captain and lieutenant. Captain Thrask gloomily forecast that if Fulton and his two associates were to be captured by the British, they would "most undoubtedly be treated as incendiaries, notwithstanding the commissions they hold from this government."[40] It is hard to imagine the usually ebullient Fulton never mentioning his new rank in any of his later correspondence. The fact that he never referred to himself as "Admiral Fulton" supports the view that he did not receive official notification of the appointment. This confusing episode was undoubtedly frustrating, and probably helped elicit the following exasperated comments from Barlow to Fulton:

> Your old idea that these fellows [French bureaucrats] are to
> be considered parts of the machine, and that you must have
> as much patience with them as with a piece of wood or
> brass, is an excellent maxim. It bears up my courage won-
> derfully every time I think of it. . . . I have told it to several
> persons, who say it is a maxim to be quoted as the mark of a

great mind. I will take care that it shall not be forgotten by the writer of your life, who, I hope, is not born yet.[41]

The *Nautilus* was transported down the Seine River to Rouen in July. Among other modifications made there was the addition of a deck twenty feet long and six feet wide to be used by the crew when cruising on the surface. On 24 July, the *Nautilus* was launched at Rouen. In underwater tests conducted five days later, the boat submerged twice in twenty-five feet of water, once for eight minutes and again for seventeen minutes. As the current of the Seine was still too strong, however, Fulton decided to move the boat to Le Havre in order to test it in the open sea. The submarine departed Rouen at six a.m. on 31 July.

Two pinnaces towed the *Nautilus* down the Seine to Le Havre, where it arrived on 4 August. Fulton spent most of that month conducting diverse experiments with his boat. On 24 August he submerged the *Nautilus* to a depth of fifteen feet. The three-man crew remained beneath the surface for more than an hour, again with only the dim light of candles for il-

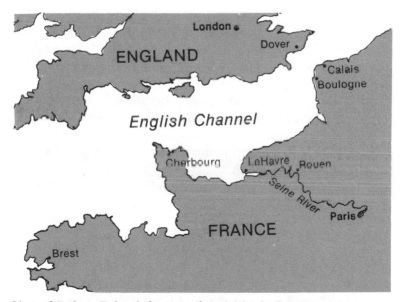

Sites of Robert Fulton's key naval activities in Europe.

lumination. Fulton and his crew spent the next day comparing two modes of surface propulsion: a propeller four feet in diameter mounted in the stern and turned manually by hand-cranks versus two men rowing oars. The propeller proved to be more powerful. On 26-27 August, Fulton experimented with depth tests and in keeping the boat in trim underwater. He successfully used a propeller mounted on a horizontal plane on the bow for this latter purpose. He also satisfactorily tested the reliability of the compass under water and experimented with an extended tube for renewing the air supply. On the twenty-seventh, Fulton tested a contact mine containing roughly 30 pounds of powder, which he used to blow up a barrel serving as a target. Satisfied with these harbor tests, Fulton felt the *Nautilus* was ready for action in the open sea. He left port on 12 September for La Hogue near Cherbourg, but after three days underway he came ashore at a spot in Normandy between what were to become the Utah and Omaha beaches of 1944 invasion fame. The *Nautilus* responded well both under water and under sail at sea. Because of gale winds, at one time she remained underwater continuously for six hours, taking in air via a metal tube that was attached permanently to the submarine. During this voyage, Fulton actually made two separate approaches on two English brigs anchored in the vicinity of the Marcou Islands. However, the ships weighed anchor and departed before he closed with them. While it is not known whether they spotted him or not, British officers had been warned as to the destructive nature of his submarine, and they were on their guard.

Ruth Barlow had accompanied Fulton to Le Havre. Always in delicate health, she felt that the sea air would be good for her. Joel Barlow remained in Paris, and evinced much concern for the well-being and safety of his younger friend in his letters to his wife. On one occasion he ruminated on the general nature of Fulton's health, making an 1800 reference to what today might be called "cloning":

Tell Toot that every strain and extraordinary exertion in
middle life, and cold and damp and twisting and wrenching

and unnatural and strained positions that our bodies are exposed to, tend to stiffen the nerves, joints and muscles, and bring on old age prematurely, perhaps sickness or decrepitude; that pains, gouts, rheumatism and death are not things of chance but are physical effects from physical causes; that the machine of his body is better and more worthy his attention than any other machine he can make: that preservation is more useful than creation; and that unless he could create me one in the image of himself he had better preserve his own automaton. Read this lecture to him, or better one, on the preservation of health and vigor, every morning at breakfast.[42]

In a more serious vein, with reference to the submarine tests, Barlow also wrote to his wife:

   . . . And poor Toot, I suppose, is now gone. I have not believed of late that there was much danger in the expedition, especially if they don't go over to the enemy's coast. I have certainly seen the day when I would have undertaken it without fear or apprehension of extraordinary risk. I can't say that I am now without uneasiness. I should probably have less if I was in the boat and without bodily pain. . . . [43]

Because of bad weather and the approaching winter, Fulton ended his tests, returned to Paris, and wrote his two friends, the prominent French mathematicians Gaspard Monge and Pierre Simon de Laplace, of his Le Havre experiments. Fulton was proud of himself, as well he should have been. He had operated a submarine extensively in the open sea in rough weather and remained submerged with his two-man crew for several hours out in the ocean. Fulton's 1800 Le Havre tests represented the most significant advancement in the development of the submarine up to this time. In November Fulton wrote his French friends a follow-up letter speculating on expenses for outfitting a submarine for sustained wartime operations. Monge and Laplace forwarded these accounts to Napoleon. They also requested an audience with the French leader in order to introduce Robert Fulton and give him an opportunity to explain his ideas first hand. Napoleon was impressed with Fulton's experiments and, on 27 November, noted that he wished to learn more about the American's naval warfare concepts.

This almost legendary meeting between Robert Fulton and Napoleon Bonaparte has been dramatized by many writers. Artists have attempted to depict it on canvas. It has even been the subject of a Saturday morning children's television show! However, it has sometimes been incorrectly believed that this meeting concerned the steamboat rather than the submarine. The exact date of their meeting is not known, but must have been between Napoleon's notation of 27 November and 3 December 1800, for on the latter date Fulton wrote that Monge and Laplace had recommended to Napoleon "dans ma presence" the authorization of 60,000 francs for the submarine project.[44]

On 4 December 1800, Forfait submitted additional data on the submarine to the First Consul. However, this time, Napoleon expressed no further personal interest in the project and ordered that "Le ministre traitera cette affaire avec Fulton, Volney et autres."[45] Thus it would appear that Napoleon wanted Forfait, Monge, Laplace and Volney, an important senator who was also one of Barlow's friends, to handle the matter.

For the next several weeks these men considered the latest information on Fulton's vessel. Monge, for example, examined a similar invention by a Swiss named Paoli and found Fulton's concept to be superior. Rather surprisingly, Forfait now objected to supporting Fulton's experiments, because he felt that Fulton was abandoning the submarine for a new interest in mine warfare. Despite his disapproval, however, the rest of the commissioners favored Fulton's project.

On 27 February 1801, Forfait advised Fulton that Napoleon approved of the project to develop the submarine. Moreover, the French government agreed to pay Fulton 10,000 francs for the purpose of conducting even more thorough tests of the *Nautilus* at the fine harbor of Brest. The American inventor was also to be given "certain sums by right of recompense," for the destruction of British warships. The amount of these sums was considerable, in particular, for that time — 400,000 francs

for ships of over thirty guns, 200,000 francs for ships of twenty
to thirty guns, and 150,000 francs for those between twelve and
twenty guns. This became official on 20 March. Robert Fulton
could not know it then, but this agreement was to represent the
apex of his negotiations with the French on his naval warfare
projects.

Forfait authorized two passports, one for Fulton and one for
a companion named Nathaniel Dargast, which granted unre-
stricted travel on French land and at sea for a period of eight
months. This designated period of time indicates that the government did not intend the Brest experiments to go on
indefinitely.

Fulton transported the *Nautilus* overland to Brest in the
spring of 1801. He spent almost two months repairing rust
damage caused by the iron bolts, which had been used instead
of copper or brass. By mid-summer he felt that the boat was
ready, and on 22 July he began his new tests. The inventor and
three companions took the *Nautilus* down to a depth of twenty-
five feet in the waters off Brest, and remained there for an
hour with no problems. Fulton did not think the *Nautilus*'s hull
would be able to withstand pressure below that depth. Two
candles provided illumination. Not satisfied with this, Fulton
modified the boat by constructing a window of dark glass top-
side near the bow. On 24 July, he found that with the new window, he had "sufficient light to count the minutes on the
watch" at a depth of twenty-five feet.[46] Fulton considered
building a total of three or four windows, to be protected by a
safety valve in case of breakage from underwater depth pressure but never built these. Two days later, he conducted successful test sailings on the surface, which included unrigging
the boat preparatory to diving. He quickly discovered that it
took only two minutes to prepare the *Nautilus* for underwater
operations. Once below the surface he further tested the compass and found it could be trusted at this new location at Brest.
Although the American inventor reckoned that the chambers
of the boat could contain enough oxygen to enable four men to
stay underwater about three hours, he wanted to lengthen this
time span. Rejecting an earlier plan to mix "carbonic acid with

lime" as being too unwieldy, he conceived of and apparently tested a system of compressed air in a portable container. On the eighth day of August, Fulton and his three companions remained beneath the surface for four hours and twenty minutes, augmenting their regular air supply with that of the portable chamber with no ill effects.

In addition to the submarine, Robert Fulton had also developed copper "submarine bombs" containing from 10 to 200 pounds of gunpowder. Each bomb would have a gunlock, i.e., a device for igniting the charge upon contact. The senior naval representative at these experiments, Admiral Villaret, authorized the use of a forty-foot sloop as target vessel for an experiment. Fulton later reported that on 12 August he commenced a run on the sloop in a surface vessel, towing a 20-pound bomb. At a distance of approximately twenty-two yards, he turned and swung the weapon into the target. The charge exploded, and the sloop was completely destroyed. Although Fulton did not indicate what type of boat he had used to make the attack, a report by the port-admiral, a man named Caffarelli, indicates that it was a pinnace, propelled by twenty-four men working four cranks. On the other hand, the well-known English diarist Joseph Farington recorded later, "When the Diving Boat approached within a quarter of a mile of it, Fulton, who was in it with 8 men at once sunk his boat. . . ."[47] It is more likely that Fulton used a pinnace as Caffarelli stated. For one thing, Farington was obviously incorrect in stationing nine men in the *Nautilus*. Secondly, Fulton had said that he "quit the experiments on the boat to try those of the Bomb Submarine."[48] Finally, he advised Edmund Cartwright of the construction details of his "pinish," stressing the need for speed.[49] There is one unresolved problem. Caffarelli's report is dated "14 Messidor an IX." This is 3 July 1801, which is more than a month before Fulton said he conducted his test; in fact, it is almost three weeks before he began tests on the *Nautilus* itself. Both Fulton and Caffarelli agreed on one point; the explosion was spectacular. Although it does not appear that the *Nautilus* was involved, the bomb test was still most important.

This was the first time a vessel had been destroyed in European waters by an underwater explosion.

Fulton spent much of the summer of 1801 cruising on the surface in the waters off Brest, looking for English ships without success. The British ships off Brest had apparently again been warned about Fulton's naval weapons. They not only had extra lookouts posted, they also stationed some of their crew in rowboats to circle their ships as an additional precaution. Fulton never had an opportunity to try his weapons. He returned to port and on 8 September he arrived in Paris, immediately advising Monge, Laplace, and Volney of his experiments at Brest. His report must have sounded very optimistic to the commission, for they told him that Napoleon wanted to see the submarine. On 20 September, however, Fulton wrote the commission a stunning letter:

> I am sorry that I had not earlier information of the (first) Counsul's [sic] desire to see the Plunging Boat. When I finished my experiments, She leaked very much and being but an imperfect engine, I did not think her further useful. — hence I took Her to pieces, Sold Her Iron work lead and cylinders and was necessitated to break the greater part of her movements in taking them to pieces. So that nothing now remains which can give an Idea of her combination; but even had She been complete I do not think She could have been brought round to Paris. . . .[50]

As if this were not enough, Fulton continued in this tone:

> . . . You will be so good as to excuse me to the Premier Consul, when I refuse to exhibit my drawings to a Committee of Engineers. For this I have two reasons; the first is not to put it in the power of anyone to explain the principles or movements lest they should pass from one to another till the enemy obtained information; the Second is that I consider this Invention as my private property, the perfectionment of which will give to France incalculable advantages over her most powerful and active enemy; and which Invention, I conceive, ought to secure to me an ample Independence. That consequently the Government should stipulate certain terms with me Before I proceed to further explanation. . . .[51]

Fulton has been accused of arrogance and chicanery because of the above letter, and not without some justification. One explanation of his behavior, however, is simply that his primary area of interest in the field of naval warfare had shifted from the submarine to his "submarine bombs." In addition, the boat had given him some problems not mentioned in his official report. Years later, he wrote from America to his old friends Monge, Laplace, and Volney:

> . . . my mode at that time for placing the submarine Bomb, or *Torpedo* under a vessel was by means of a submarine boat, in which boat I navigated under water but finding her extremely difficult to manage I have abandoned her. Instead of which I have by reflection and Experiment found a certain and very simple method for fixing the Torpedos to a ship and sending them Under her bottom whether she be at Anchor or under sail. . . .[52]

The American inventor had first become interested in underwater explosives during his 1800 Le Havre tests. As noted, he experimented in blowing up a floating barrel with what he called a "torpedo." Again, the main inspiration for this device seems to have been the work of David Bushnell. After the *Turtle* episode, Bushnell began to work on floating explosive charges. In August 1777, Bushnell transmitted a floating bomb from a small boat in the direction of a British naval ship off New London, Connecticut. It missed the main target, but hit a small boat, killing the three British sailors on board. In late December 1777, Bushnell dispatched a number of floating explosives down the Delaware River from Bordentown, New Jersey, towards the British ships moored near Philadelphia. However, Bushnell misjudged the speed of the current, and by the time the explosives reached the general locale of the target, most of the British ships had departed. Unfortunately, two young American boys were killed while playing with one of the devices. The writer Francis Hopkinson commemorated this exercise in futility the following year in his satirical poem "The Battle of the Kegs."

Although Bushnell preferred the term "magazine" to de-

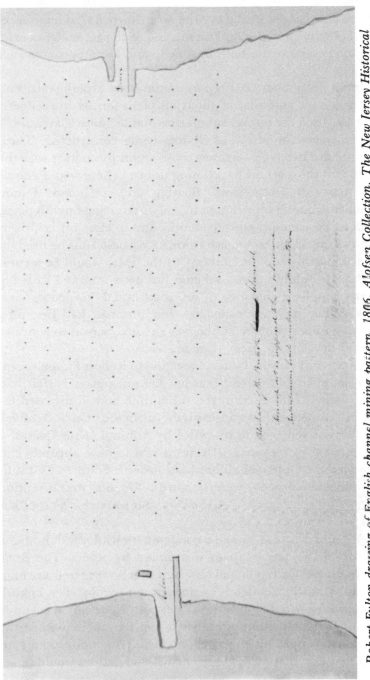

Robert Fulton drawing of English channel mining pattern, 1805. Alofsen Collection, The New Jersey Historical Society, Alan Frazer, photographer

scribe his weapon, he did use the term "torpedo" at least once, in 1778, thus antedating Fulton's use of the term. Of course, the modern name for both Bushnell's and Fulton's contrivance is "mine."

In his September 1801 report on the Brest experiments, Fulton was most enthusiastic about his plans for his "torpedoes." (He also used the terms "Submarine Bombs" and "Carcasses.") He envisaged hundreds of devices being constructed. These would have two types of fuses, those set off by contact with the ship, and those set off by a timing device. There would also be two types of "torpedoes," floating and anchored. Fulton planned on using his weapons to seal up strategic English ports, such as Portsmouth and Plymouth, and to close off key rivers such as the Thames. English commerce would thus be brought to a standstill, and the "Liberty of the Seas" would be secure. Although Fulton's grand scheme has been attacked as being overly simplistic, his idea of using anchored "torpedoes" was new. While it is acknowledged that Bushnell had first used floating mines, Robert Fulton was the first person to conceive of and develop the moored mine.

Minister of Marine Forfait's reaction to Robert Fulton's arrogant letter of 20 September is not known, but as Forfait had been largely interested in the submarine and ill-disposed towards "torpedoes," it can easily be surmised. On 1 October, Forfait was replaced in his office by Admiral Denis Decres, a more conservative officer. Decres is said to have abruptly and completely terminated all negotiations with Fulton on his submarine and "torpedo" with the words, "Go, Sir, your invention is good for the Algerians or Corsairs, but learn that France has not yet abandoned the ocean."[53]

Admiral Decres's implicit condemnation of the inhumane nature of the new weapons was shared by others. The Brest port-admiral Caffarelli had observed that no true military man would want to meet death by underwater bombs. The English also condemned Fulton's naval weapons. The noted scientist Count Benjamin Rumford advised Joel Barlow that while the submarine appeared effective, "no civilized nation would consent to use it; that men, governments, and nations would fight, and that it was better for morals and general happiness of all people that the fighting should be done on land."[54] Robert Livingston, soon to become Robert Fulton's steamboat partner, defended Fulton against Rumford. Livingston stated that the submarine would be used to end naval wars and achieve liberty of the seas and that he was so sure of the submarine's ultimately humane purpose that he had recommended it to the American government. Other Americans did not agree with Livingston. The Gloucester sea captain, Israel Thrask, was a friend of Fulton's assistant Nathaniel Sergeant. Thrask wrote: "My heart aches for poor Sargent [sic]. . . . This leads me to a sad reflection — that a man of the best heart in the world is subject to be driven by a long continuance of adverse fortune and dire necessity to embrace objects that his very nature, in a different situation, would revolt at."[55]

According to Napoleon's private secretary, sometime in 1801 the First Consul had said of Fulton, "Bah, these projectors are all either intriguers or visionaries. Don't trouble me about the business."[56] Another translation of the same speech indicates that Napoleon also said of Fulton, "Don't mention him again."[57] Although neither the month nor the date of Napoleon's disparaging comments is recorded, both sources do agree on the year. This would, therefore, disprove the often noted allegation that Napoleon was speaking of Fulton's steamboat, as Fulton did not try to contact Napoleon on that new enterprise until 1803. There were probably at least two reasons for Napoleon's disenchantment with Fulton and his naval weapons. First, he was probably understandably angry with Fulton for destroying his submarine, thereby denying Napoleon's engineers a chance to copy it. Second, Napoleon's diplomats were actively engaged in negotiations with the British which would ultimately result in the Peace of Amiens of 1802, and Bonaparte could have felt that French patronage of Fulton and his inventions would have been too provocative to Britain.

As it turned out, in 1809, Napoleon did authorize a French firm to build a submarine at Le Havre.[58] There is also a rather fantastic story not fully authenticated, that an English adventurer concocted a scheme to rescue Napoleon from St. Helena in a submarine in 1821, but the former French leader died before the vessel was completed.[59]

After the rejection of his submarine and mines by the French authorities, Fulton busied himself with other activities. He continued to paint and had his own likeness sketched by the young American artist, John Vanderlyn. From April to September 1802, Fulton again escorted Ruth Barlow on an extended vacation while her husband stayed behind in Paris. Mrs. Barlow's health had not improved, so, accompanied by Fulton, she went to partake of the medicinal waters at Plombieres in the Vosges mountain region. Barlow was envious. He wrote to them: "I almost see the little whites [horses] now trudging along this fine morning and turning back their short ears to hear wife and Toot talking about Hub, and then they stop and laugh to hear her say, 'Come, Lazybones, get out and walk up the hill; see how steep it is: if Hub was here he would walk up every one of these hills. . . . ' Oh, I wish I was there."[60] Fulton was engaged during this rustic sojourn in drawing sketches for Barlow's *Columbiad*. He appears to have been quite concerned with minute details, for on one occasion, Barlow responded to a request from him for information on Washington's and Cornwallis's hats. More significantly, Barlow and Fulton's correspondence indicated that Robert Fulton was becoming increasingly interested in a new project—the steamboat.

Many well-intentioned fourth-grade teachers to the contrary, Robert Fulton did not exactly "invent" the steamboat. It is very difficult, if not impossible, to state who did. The first person verified to have moved a boat by steam was the Marquis de Jouffroy, who in 1783 operated a 140-foot-long steamboat with paddlewheels on the Saone River at Lyons, France. However, Jouffroy's boiler and, indeed, his entire vessel broke up after fifteen minutes operation. William Henry, a gun manufacturer from Lancaster, Pennsylvania, is said to have built a "steamboat" in Conestoga Creek in 1763, but there is no direct evidence of this.

The work of John Fitch and James Rumsey in the United States in the 1780s represented a significant advancement in the development of a functional steamboat. Each of these men independently designed and constructed a working steamboat, Fitch's achievement being the more impressive of the two. In 1786 this former Connecticut clockmaker built a rather strange vessel motivated by twelve long paddles, six on each side, which were driven by steam. While the vessel did function, it apparently broke down a lot. In August 1787, however, John Fitch built and operated a substantially new steamboat, which made several impressive demonstrations at Philadelphia to an audience that included several members of the Constitutional Convention. Fitch modified the boat to provide greater power, and by 1790 his vessel was operating technically successfully on the Delaware. Moreover, the boat attained a speed of eight miles an hour and was soon carrying passengers back and forth from Burlington, New Jersey, to Philadelphia, stopping at key towns in between. During the summer of 1790, Fitch's boat traversed almost 3,000 miles with very few breakdowns. Unfortunately, few people used this service, and Fitch was finally forced out of business. This was a classic case of an idea being introduced before its time had come. Despite his adversity, Fitch somehow maintained a sense of humor. In 1792 he wrote to a friend: " . . . I wish to expend three or four dollars more on the Steam Boat and if successful to have Six or seven to take me to some place of retirement. I therefore seriously request you lend me Ten Dollars, and if I am an honest man you shall have no cause to complain if not the Loss cannot be great. . . . "[61] Frustrated and unappreciated, John Fitch died of a combination of alcohol and opium in 1798.

Working on his own, James Rumsey experimented with a primitive steamboat near present-day Shepherdstown, West Virginia, on the Potomac in December 1787. While the boat performed satisfactorily, it was operated only twice and was then abandoned. Rumsey's experiments attracted some important backers, who included George Washington. Rumsey went to England in 1788, worked on a new steamboat there, and died in 1792. The next year his English partners tested his boat, apparently successfully, in an experimental run at four miles an hour.

Following the important work of John Fitch and James

Rumsey, several other Americans made contributions to the development of the steamboat before Dobert Fulton's historic voyage up the Hudson in 1807. Among these were William Longstreet, Samuel Morey, Nathan Read, John Stevens, Nicholas J. Roosevelt, Robert E. Livingston, and Oliver Evans. In addition, one Englishman's work in particular was very important. William Symington made a trial run of an early steamboat model in 1788 in Scotland with poet Robert Burns on board. Later in 1802-03 Symington built a steam tugboat called the *Charlotte Dundas*, which operated on the Firth of Forth and Clyde Canal in Scotland for a brief period.

Although there is little evidence in original sources, it is possible that some of these older inventors may have influenced Fulton. The inventor William Henry was from Lancaster, Pennsylvania, and he may have met Fulton there. During his visit to Bath, Virginia, in 1786, Fulton could also have viewed Rumsey's steamboat while it was being constructed. Prior to his

Bronze replica of Houdon's plaster cast of Robert Fulton, 1803. National Portrait Gallery, Smithsonian Institution

departure from England, Fulton returned from Bath to Philadelphia, where it is possible that he observed Fitch's initial experiments. Once in England, Fulton and Rumsey could con-
ceivably have met again, as Rumsey's good friend was a fellow
student of Fulton's at Benjamin West's studio. It has also been
alleged that Fulton saw some of Symington's earlier experiments, but this has been hard to prove. In France, Fulton was
certainly familiar with Fitch's work, as there is a copy of an entry from John Fitch's diary dating from that period in Robert
Fulton's hand, presently in the Montague Collection of the Fulton papers at the New York Public Library. Oliver Evans met
Fulton in France, and the two Americans could possibly have
exchanged technical ideas of mutual interest.

Robert Fulton certainly could not have conceived of the
steamboat as he did without his predecessors' examples, however, his work was the most significant. The combination of
parts in his steamboat was the most successful, and the use and
development of the steamboat began in earnest after his successful 1807 Hudson run. The relationship of his two most important predecessors, John Fitch and James Rumsey, to Fulton
can best be compared to that of John Wycliffe and John Hus,
forerunners of the Reformation, to Martin Luther, "Father of
the Reformation." Let Thomas Jefferson have the last word on
this subject:

> . . . Who invented the steamboat? Was it Gerbert, the
> Marquis of Worcester, Newcomen, Savery, Papin, Fitch,
> Fulton? The fact is, that one new idea leads to another, that
> to a third, and so on through a course of time until some
> one, with whom no one of these ideas is original, combines
> all together, and produces what is justly called a new
> invention.[62]

Robert Fulton began to actively pursue his interest in steamboats in England in 1793. Earl Stanhope was also working in
this area, and he and his new American friend often exchanged ideas. Fulton laconically wrote to him, "In June 1793
I began the experiments of the steam-ship. My first design was
to imitate the spring in the tail of a salmon."[63] The following

year while in Manchester Fulton requested the firm of Boulton and Watt to provide him with prices for a three or four-horsepower engine for possible use in a steamboat. Nothing developed from his inquiry at this time. Fulton also discussed steamboats with power loom inventor Edmund Cartwright. The two men continued their discourse on steamboats through considerable correspondence after Fulton departed for France in 1797.[64] Fulton's most important work on the steamboat in England was the result of an order for a design from the Duke of Bridgewater. Fulton complied, and the boat was eventually constructed by others and completed although it is not certain if it was ever operational. It was christened, ironically in view of Fulton's later activities, the *Buonaparte*.

In 1803, Fulton formed a partnership with the American Robert Livingston to develop his steamboat. The position, money, political influence, and style that Livingston brought with him as Fulton's partner were most important to the eventual success of Fulton's project. In 1797 Fulton had written Cartwright, "I have a great objection to partners. I never would have but one if I could help it, and that should be a wife."[65] Five years later Livingston was able to write home: "You know my passion for steam boats & the money I have expended on that object—I am not yet discouraged and tho all my old partners have given up the pursuit I have found a new one in Robert Fulton a most ingenious young man the inventor of the diving boat which has made so much noise in Europe. . . . "[66] In 1798 Livingston had experimented with steamboats in New Jersey in partnership with John Stevens and Nicholas J. Roosevelt. Livingston was appointed minister plenipotentiary to France by President Jefferson in 1801, and, at the time of his partnership with Fulton, was about to negotiate the Louisiana Purchase, along with James Monroe. Joel Barlow first introduced Fulton to Livingston, but he had some misgivings about the partnership. Barlow did not quite trust the New York chancellor and would have preferred to see his young friend aligned with Daniel Parker, another American with whom Barlow had business connections. Fulton did not care for Parker, and Barlow reluctantly acquiesced.[67]

With his new partner, Robert Fulton set to work on his steamboat design. He had some difficulty determining what was the best mechanism for propelling the boat and was not convinced that the stern paddles of his earlier English design were the answer. For a time he favored oars.[68] His old friend Tom Paine was no help; he suggested that Fulton use gunpowder to propel the vessel! After much experimentation, Fulton settled on paddlewheels on each side and built a small model. Then, after some initial difficulty, he constructed a boat approximately seventy feet long, equipped with an eight-horsepower engine. The trial run was conducted in Paris 9 August 1803. According to a contemporary scientific report, Fulton and three assistants left the quay on the Seine at six p.m. on the ninth. He tested the boat and engine both upstream and downstream for an hour and a half. Outside of the boat's lack of speed, the run was generally successful. Back in 1802 while at Plombières, Fulton had sketched a plan for a steamboat run from New York to Albany on the Hudson River. He was now ready to implement this plan, although it would be delayed by three more years of work on his naval warfare inventions in France and England.

Fulton now decided to present to Napoleon a plan for using his steamboat in naval warfare. Following the breakdown of the Peace of Amiens in 1803, the French leader had determined to invade England. As the French writer and critic of Napoleon, Madame de Stael, facetiously put it, "During the summer of 1803 began the great farce of the invasion of England."[69] Early in September 1803, Fulton's old contact Forfait advised Napoleon that the American inventor wanted to again see the First Consul (now First Consul for life), this time to discuss both his political ideas and his "new endeavors."[70] The American inventor wanted to propose to Napoleon that he sponsor a fleet of Fulton-designed steamboats to transport his military forces from the port of Boulogne across the Channel in the invasion of England. Napoleon referred the matter to the Academy of Sciences, but privately did not appear to care much for Fulton's proposal. He wrote to his foreign minister Talleyrand from Boulogne, "The affair . . . does not merit

much attention. For a great length of time people have occupied themselves with the means of propelling boats without
men."[71] The scientists did not report favorably on Fulton's
plan, and Napoleon dropped the matter without having seen
the inventor. The chancellor of France, Etienne-Denis Duc
Pasquier, sadly observed of Napoleon:

> . . . Never was he more badly served by his instinct. What
> might he not have been able to accomplish, had he been the
> first to avail himself of this new means of reaching his most
> mortal enemy? . . . Surprise will doubtless be felt that a
> genius, such as that of the First Consul's, should not have at
> once grasped the range of the offer made him by Fulton.[72]

However, Pasquier did doubt, justifiably, that Fulton would be
able to build enough steamboats in time for the invasion. But
the French chancellor also was looking towards the future and
felt that Napoleon had lacked foresight by dismissing Fulton's
idea altogether.

Fulton might have saved himself further frustration if he had
paid more attention to his steamboat partner's observations on
Napoleon. One year before, Robert Livingston had warned
Secretary of State James Madison:

> . . . There never was a Government in which less could be
> done by negotiation than here. There is no people, no
> Legislature, no counsellors. One man is everything. He
> seldom asks advice, and never hears it unasked. His ministers
> are mere clerks; and his Legislature and counsellors parade
> officers. . . . [73]

Napoleon changed his appraisal of Fulton drastically in
1804. Apparently the scientists whom he had casually placed in
charge of investigating Fulton's steamboat invasion scheme
had finally filled him in on the details. Napoleon wrote ex-
citedly on 21 July 1804 that he had just read Fulton's proposi-
tion, and that he believed that "it could change the face of the
world."[74]

The French leader hurriedly convened a new commission to
seriously pursue the matter, but it was too late. Robert Fulton

had departed from France. Fulton had offered France submarines to attack British ships, mines to close off British ports and rivers, and finally, steamboats to transport French troops to England. All his inventions had been rejected, however, and the opportunity for the French had passed. Robert Fulton had now left that country forever for the camp of her mortal enemy.

3

A Sojourn in Britain, 1804–1806

In April 1804 Robert Fulton left France and returned to England, where he was to spend more than two years, mainly working on the development of his naval weapons. Although his submarine experiments were to end with the British government's rejection of this invention, during this time he was to make significant contributions in the field of mine warfare.

The British had known about Robert Fulton's experiments with underwater weapons since 1798. In that year Joshua Gilpin told Earl Stanhope of his American friend's activities. Among other things, Gilpin said of Fulton, "the [French] Government and he are amusing each other (I think however to little purpose) on his new invention of the submarine boat. I fear this will keep him from more useful pursuits."[1] Stanhope was apparently not very much concerned at first with Gilpin's report. Four years later, however, Fulton himself wrote to his old English companion and brought him up to date on the progress of his submarine. Fulton's news greatly alarmed Stanhope, who, despite his feelings for his American friend, prepared to deliver a ringing warning to the House of Lords on this possible threat to England. On 13 May 1802, Stanhope requested that the galleries be cleared, stressing the need for secrecy concerning the matter he was about to discuss. Apparently he extravagantly described the new naval invention as being "brought to perfection by a person in France as to render the destruction of ships absolutely sure . . . and that there was no way of preventing it."[2] Stanhope had overstated his case, to say the least. Fulton may not have had much luck with the French, but by 1802 his submarine was certainly impressing the British.

Stanhope continued to warn others in private. Several months later, he informed the influential and noted diarist Joseph Farington of Fulton's 1801 submarine experiments off Brest. Farington wrote in his diary that "this most dangerous & dreadful contrivance is said to be fully understood only by Fulton."[3] Another of Fulton's prominent English friends, Edmund Cartwright, was also aroused by this potential threat to his country. The British government consulted with Cartwright, among others, in developing contingency plans should Fulton's weapon be used against England. The Admiralty Office sent a secret circular to the top naval operational commanders, warning them to be on the lookout for an enemy submarine. This intelligence report mentions Fulton by name and stressed the threat to the "Ships and Vessels in the Port of London."[4]

Henry Addington, Lord Sidmouth, became head of the government in 1801. By the spring of 1803, Addington had become so impressed with the submarine reports that he opened negotiations with the American inventor in an attempt to induce him to come over to England. Stanhope, in one of his official consultations, may have advised Addington as to the probability of success in such a venture.

The first phase of the Addington-Fulton negotiations has all the drama of a modern espionage novel. Fulton was living in a country with which England was at war; the Peace of Amiens had failed, and the conflict between France and England had resumed in May 1803. Initially, therefore, the English had to approach Fulton covertly. The records do not reveal the name of the intermediary chosen for this task. One of Fulton's major biographers identifies this contact as a "Dr. Gregory," but Fulton says he was "an english Gentlemen in London who had known me for some years in Paris," and an acquaintance of Dr. Gregory's.[5] This "English gentleman," never identified further, assumed the name "Smith" and met secretly with Fulton in

Paris in 1803. Adding to the melodramatic quality of these proceedings, Fulton operated under the name of "Robert Francis" and continued to do so throughout most of his dealings with London for the next few years.

"Mr. Smith" told "Mr. Francis" that England wanted to employ his submarine against the French. Fulton was skeptical at first, as he did not believe that it was in England's interest as a major naval power to use such craft against a lesser naval force. Also, he wanted to see some written proof of the British offer, but "Mr. Smith" told Fulton that it would be too dangerous to carry papers of that sort. Ohe Englishman did have, however, 800 pounds for travel expenses for both men back to England. As Fulton was almost always in financial straits, it can be imagined that his opposition lessened somewhat on hearing this news. Still, he was not altogether convinced, so he prepared an extensive list of proposals for "Smith" to carry back to England. The key point of this list was that Fulton was willing to explain fully both his submarine and his "Submarine Bombs" in return for the payment of one hundred thousand pounds sterling. Robert Fulton had certainly increased his estimation of what his naval inventions were worth.

"Mr. Smith" returned to England with Fulton's offer. Because the two men felt that it would be too hazardous to meet again in Paris, they agreed that Fulton should go to Holland and wait for "Smith" to contact him there. Fulton accordingly traveled to Amsterdam, apparently over exceedingly bad roads, in the latter part of 1803. Upon arriving in the Dutch city, his old interest in canals was reawakened. He wrote to a friend:

> After much josteling [sic] over roads which disgrace nations called civilized from Antwerp to Rotterdam I arrived by land and water to this famous City where many a black canal bears on its sable bosome [sic] the ponderous merchandise. . . . In Rome in the time of Agrippa it is said a great part of the ponderous carriage of the city passed through the Subterranean Aqueduct, and I once had the same Idea for a plan which I mean to propose one day for cities in America, but would not open canals be better?[6]

Weeks passed with no word from "Mr. Smith." Fulton busied himself by traveling around Holland, by painting, and by following up an order he had made previously for an engine for his steamboat. On 6 August 1803 while still in Paris, Fulton had written to the Birmingham firm of Boulton and Watt requesting them to build a twenty-four-horsepower engine for use on a steamboat in the United States. On 4 October, the English company replied that they would not be able to accept the contract to built the engine, because they had been unable to obtain their government's permission to ship the engine to America. Not giving up, Fulton wrote letters from Rotterdam and later from Paris to the recently installed American minister in London, James Monroe, requesting aid in obtaining a permit to ship the engine home. Monroe finally answered Fulton early in 1804 and said he could do nothing. Fulton wrote back on 4 March 1804:

> . . . As the Steam Engine is realy [*sic*] designed for a Steam
> Boat and has no connexion with any of my other mechanical
> Experiments . . . the British Government must have little
> friendship or even civility towards America if they refuse
> such a request. If you suppose their objection is based on any
> act of mine and it would be well that my name should not
> appear you will be so good as to demand permission . . . for
> Mr. Livingston. . . .[7]

It is possible that the British government's refusal of an engine export permit was an attempt to pressure Fulton in their negotiations on his naval weapons. They may also have been fearful that if they granted Fulton the permit, he would leave their country before giving them a chance to acquire his weapons. However, it is more likely that the British were denying Fulton permission because, in general, they discouraged all exportation of their industrial and technological ideas. In the previous century, Samuel Slater, the Englishman regarded as the founder of the American industrial revolution, had circumvented this policy by memorizing the plans of British machines and then establishing a textile mill in Rhode Island.

"Mr. Smith" never did come and meet with Fulton in Holland. "Mr. Francis" returned to Paris, and the Englishman contacted him there, this time carrying a letter from British Foreign Secretary Lord Hawkesbury. In this letter, the Secretary indicated that Fulton's price of one hundred thousand pounds would not be considered until the inventions were examined and tested in England. However, Hawkesbury emphasized that if Fulton trusted England with his naval concepts, he would be treated *"with the utmost liberality and Generosity."*[8] A leading diplomatic historian has said that Hawkesbury was particularly well disposed towards the United States[9] and perhaps Fulton took that into consideration. In any case, Hawkesbury's letter decided the issue for him, and Fulton soon left Paris and reached England in April 1804.

As soon as he arrived in London, Fulton contacted the government with a personal request for the steam engine export permit. The British cagily issued a permit authorizing construction of the engine but indicated that a permit for exportation would not be considered until Fulton had made final his plans for leaving England. Fulton was going to have to stay in England for a while.

Just before Fulton's arrival in England, Addington resigned as chief minister, and in May 1804 once again the great William Pitt was selected to guide the British government. Hawkesbury, though succeeded by Lord Harrowby as foreign secretary, remained in the cabinet in another post. A lackluster but pro-American ministry was being replaced by one much more energetic, but also more inimical to the interests of America and individual Americans.

Fulton's correspondence during May and June 1804 indicates that his major contact in the government at this time was a Mr. Hammond. That this was George Hammond, under secretary of state for the Foreign Department, is confirmed by a letter written in 1805 by Viscount Castlereagh, then secretary of war. Classified "most secret" and subsequently released by the Admiralty, this letter authorized Under Secretary of State George Hammond to settle certain financial questions with "Mr. Francis."[10]

Fulton did not plan to let the change in ministries affect

negotiations on his naval weapons. On 22 May, he told the Pitt government that it must appoint a special commission to examine his inventions. While in France, Fulton had argued that the mode of naval warfare he envisaged would be much better suited to a weak naval power like France than to a strong naval force like the Royal Navy. Now in England, he changed his reasoning, writing Pitt: "I beg leave to propose (a plan) which will be prompt in execution and if Successful will forever Remove from the mind of Man the possibility of France making a descent on England. I propose a submarine expedition to destroy the fleets of Boulogne and Brest as they now lie. . . ."[11] Fulton demanded a salary of 200 pounds a month while engaged in this endeavor. This was to be in addition to his original request for a flat 100,000 pounds.

Just a few months earlier, Robert Fulton had offered his naval weapons and concepts to Napoleon for use against England. Now he was proposing to destroy the same military force he had hoped to ferry across the English Channel in his steamboats! Two important twentieth-century commentators feel that Fulton's startling reversal of loyalties was largely based on his growing dislike of Napoleon for his betrayal of the general ideals of liberty, equality, and fraternity of the French Revolution.[12] In 1804, Beethoven angrily changed the dedication of his Third Symphony from a tribute to Napoleon to the more generalized tribute, the "Eroica." In like manner, in the same year Fulton replaced his allegiance to Napoleon with a more generalized concern: opposition to tyranny. There is some justification for this view. In the days before 18 Brumaire, the French date of Napoleon's coup d'etat, Fulton had felt an engineer's kinship with the rising artillery specialist. That he no longer felt that sympathy is illustrated by a discourse Fulton delivered early in 1805 entitled "Observations on Bonaparte's Pacific Communications," in which he wrote of the "Little Corporal":

> Raised from nothing by military talents and a combination of extriordinary [sic] events, he is intoxicated with success, adulation has become his daily food as necessary to his happiness as high seasoning to a vitiated appetite. . . . he seeks

to be ranked by the future historian above Ceasar [*sic*] and Charlemagne, his principle is that future ages never take into consideration the miseries which accompany war, they only listen to the brilliant actions of the Chief. . . .[13]

Other facts, however, conflict with the above argument. In 1806 diarist Joseph Farington reported that Fulton had told him "that Buonaparte who had done so much for the *glory* of that Country . . . is and cannot be otherways than popular. Besides who else have they to look to?"[14] Later, in 1811, back in the United States, Fulton would send an agent back to France to attempt to reinterest Napoleon in his naval warfare inventions.[15] Fulton's disapprobation of Napoleon in 1804 most likely was based on a combination of realistic and idealistic considerations. On the one hand, Fulton needed money and was tired of French inaction. On the other, he quite probably did believe in his often stated desire to secure liberty of the seas with his naval weapons. Fulton directly addressed this subject in his 1810 publication *Torpedo War and Submarine Explosions*:

> . . . I may be accused of enmity to England and partiality to France; yet I have neither hatred nor particular attachment to any foreign country. I admire the ingenuity, industry, and good faith of the English people; I respect the arts, sciences and amiable manners of the people of France. . . . But my feelings are wholly attached to my country . . . I am happy that the liberty of the seas will not only benefit America; it will be an immense advantage to England, to France, and to every other nation. . . .[16]

Robert Fulton's technical concept of the submarine had changed since the Brest operations of 1801. At some point during his first months in England, he made a drawing of a small submarine which he named the "Messenger." This submarine was to be nine feet long, thus large enough for one man only, but it was never constructed.[17] More significantly, Fulton was also planning a craft thirty-five feet long, ten feet wide, and eight feet deep.[18] This would be a little larger than the *Nautilus*, which had been twenty-one feet four inches by seven feet. Fulton wanted to design a boat that could sustain a crew of six for twenty days at sea and be anchored while submerged. It is difficult to say whether this submarine would have been an improvement over the old *Nautilus* as, like the "Messenger," it was never built.

Fulton did not quietly await the British government's decision on his proposal of 22 May, but instead sent them a list of names to be recommended for appointment to the proposed commission. As might be expected, his old friends, Stanhope and Cartwright, were included on his list. Unfortunately for Fulton, they were not part of the board finally appointed by the government. Nevertheless, the commission selected was very impressive, its members being Sir Joseph Banks, the president of the Royal Society; Sir Home Popham, a distinguished naval officer; John Rennie and Henry Cavendish, two distinguished scientists; and Major William Congreve, inventor of the Congreve rocket, whose "red glare" during the 1814 British bombardment of Fort McHenry at Baltimore would be immortalized by Francis Scott Key in "The Star-Spangled Banner." Fulton especially liked Home Popham and Congreve, whom he would later describe as his friends and companions. He could also be pleased in particular with the choice of Banks, as the American inventor was sometimes invited to breakfast in the li-

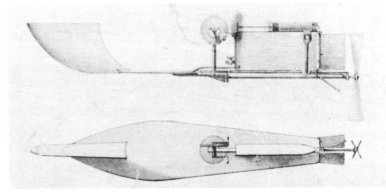

Robert Fulton drawing of his one-man submarine "Messenger," which was never built, no date. Alofsen Collection, The New Jersey Historical Society, Alan Frazer, photographer

brary of Sir Joseph, a wealthy patron of distinguished scientists.

The board quickly considered Fulton's proposals. Without consulting him, it determined that while his submarine vessel was probably technically feasible, it most likely would prove impracticable in combat. With this report, Robert Fulton's work on the submarine in Europe was to end. Fulton may have had intimations of the committee's unfavorable proceedings, for on 6 June he wrote directly to William Pitt, apparently so agitated that he revealed his true identity: ". . . Robert Fulton known by the name of Francis Author of Submarine Navigation. . . . I beg 20 minuets [*sic*] conversation with you as soon as possible."[19] Even before receiving an answer, Fulton wrote a letter of complaint to Under Secretary of State Hammond, stating in part,

> The first day I had the pleasure of seeing you I promised you candor and should time make me more known to your government they will find frankness one of the leading lines of my character. Now I candidly declare that having been here 5 weeks in some degree like a prisoner and at present as

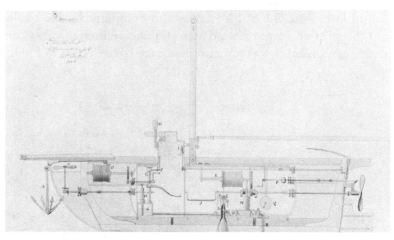

Robert Fulton drawing of his second, more sophisticated submarine, which was unnamed and never built, 1806. Alofsen Collection, The New Jersey Historical Society, Alan Frazer, photographer

much in the dark as on the day of my arrival such a state of suspense begins to grow extremely unpleasant.[20]

Shortly after this, the American received word of the board's unfavorable decision on the submarine.

Fulton continued to write agitated letters to Hammond, Home Popham, and others. A chance meeting with an old acquaintance may also have aided Fulton in his search for support of his naval concepts. One night, while at the opera in London, Fulton spotted a familiar face in the box above him. It was the young noblewoman he had gallantly tried to rescue from the French authorities in Calais in 1797 with an offer of marriage. He had seen her once since then, in Paris, but had again been confused by her mysterious manner. Now, she beckoned him to her box and, after introducing him to her circle of elegant companions, told him the full story of her secretive and mysterious behavior during the dangerous days of the French Revolution. At first Fulton reacted animatedly, saying, "Oh dear me! This is too much! She is always changing her name! It is enough to drive one mad!" However, after she explained that her name was actually the Duchess de Gontaut, and that her aristocratic background necessitated that she travel in France under an assumed name, Fulton finally understood, and said good-naturedly, "I congratulate your husband on having a wife who at one time was on the point of turning my head or of sending me to the devil!" This encounter was important in that Fulton met one of the Duchess's companions, the influential Lord Clarendon. According to the duchess, Lord Clarendon soon became good friends with Fulton and introduced him to many key government officials and scientists.[21] Fulton's perseverance was finally rewarded. William Pitt invited him to breakfast at his country house on 20 July 1804, in company with Home Popham. At this meeting, plans for Fulton's "torpedoes" were discussed, and at last a contract was produced and signed. This success did not come as a complete surprise to Fulton as he had been corresponding extensively with Home Popham on the subject, and his hunch re-

garding the considerable influence of the aristocratic naval
officer had been correct.

This contract of 20 July 1804 was to be the basis for all of
Robert Fulton's ensuing naval activities in England. The major
features of this important document were: Fulton agreed to explain the principles of attacking a fleet with "submarine
Bombs" to the British, as well as to supervise the execution of
such an operation; he would receive 200 pounds a month while
so employed; up to 7,000 pounds would be set aside for "the
payment of his mechanical preparations"; "His Majesty's Dock
Yards and Arsenals" would furnish all materials; Fulton would
received 40,000 pounds for every decked French vessel destroyed by his weapons; "When government has no further occasion for his service . . . then he is only to be paid one quarter
of the supposed value of such vessels as may be destroyed by his

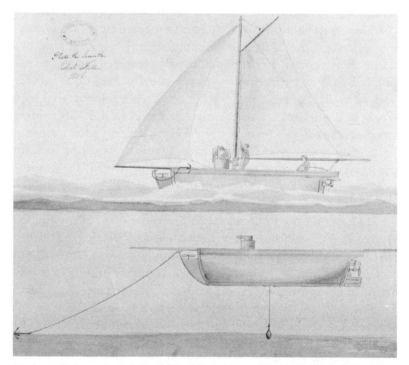

*Robert Fulton drawing of his submarine, 1806. Alofsen Collection,
The New Jersey Historical Society, Alan Frazer, photographer*

scheme"; and, most significantly, if the government were to find itself unable to carry out Fulton's plan due to political or other considerations, but after testing found it to be "practicable and . . . a more effective mode of destroying the enemies fleet at Boulogne, Brest, or elsewhere, than any now in practice and with less risk," then Fulton would be paid 40,000 pounds for having demonstrated the effectiveness of his weapons.[22]

Robert Fulton now had British authorization to proceed with his "torpedo" experiments. The first opportunity to employ his weapons in actual combat would present itself sooner than he knew. At almost the very moment that Fulton's English contract was signed and delivered, Napoleon was in Paris dictating the following words to one of his ranking officers: "Our situation with regard to England is most favourable. . . . I have at my disposal nearly 120,000 men and 3,000 launches, etc., which only wait a favourable wind in order to plant the imperial eagle on the tower of London. Time & destiny alone know what will happen."[23]

Napoleon had amassed hundreds of warships at Boulogne and the Channel ports to invade England, spurring the English to intensify their preparations to counter the French attack. The British naval operational commander, Lord Keith, was preparing a large-scale naval operation against the French invasion force. Robert Fulton supervised the construction of twenty mines for the mission. He described his mines as "5 large coffers, 5 small, and 10 hogsheads," and told Keith, "I hope (they) will be sufficient to enable your Lordship to give a good account at Boulogne."[24] Home Popham kept a close watch on the proceedings and told Keith that Fulton's "New Curiosities" would be ready shortly.

The seldom retiring Fulton did not plan to let Lord Keith alone manage the Boulogne mission. The American inventor intended to intercept the English flotilla on 23 September. Then, after a training session the next day, he hoped the actual attack would begin on the night of 25 September. Although Fulton succeeded in joining the fleet, Keith had other plans for the attack. From the deck of the HMS *Monarch*,

French drawing of Fulton's delivery craft for the mines used in the raid on Boulogne. Smithsonian Institution

Keith delayed the assault on the French fleet until 2 October, waiting for favorable weather. He began the operation at 9:15 p.m. which lasted until 4:15 the following morning.

The plan of attack was to approach the enemy ships in small boats, carrying the mines. Fulton had begun to experiment with a new technique for delivering his mines that he now tried in this foray. This method consisted of attaching two mines to a line, one at each end, before setting their timing mechanisms and throwing them overboard. Fulton hoped that, as the mines drifted with the tide, their connecting line would wrap itself around the enemy ship's anchor cable. As a ship normally rides downwind of its anchor cable, the mines would then be carried near the target by the tide, where their positions would be secured by the attached line, which would prevent them from drifting away or bypassing the target. That the bobbing attached casks sometimes gave the impression of being small, twin-hulled craft (known as catamarans) is the most plausible reason for the 1804 Boulogne raid sometimes being referred to as the "Catamaran Expedition." However, the most often cited reason for this designation is a poem that appeared in the 27 October 1804 issue of *Cobbett's Political Register*. Written by the English political writer William Cobbett, this popular satirical work described the delivery craft as being nearly submerged catamarans, containing cold, wet sailors lying in water up to their chins.

A participant in this raid, John Allison of the HMS *Leopard* (this ship's famous role in American history three years later is described earlier in this book in "The War of 1807"), described what actually happened:

> I proceeded with two casks in the Leopard's long cutter, one in the bow, the other in the stern sheets; stood inshore and made the round battery to the southward. I dropped down until I could plainly see the flotilla, and driving directly for them by the tide, at the distance of about half a cable, I took the pin out of the aftermost cask. . . . I put my ear to the machinery and heard it going, then ordered it to be thrown overboard and told Mr. Gilbert . . . to take the pin out of the cask in the bow. They answered it was out. I

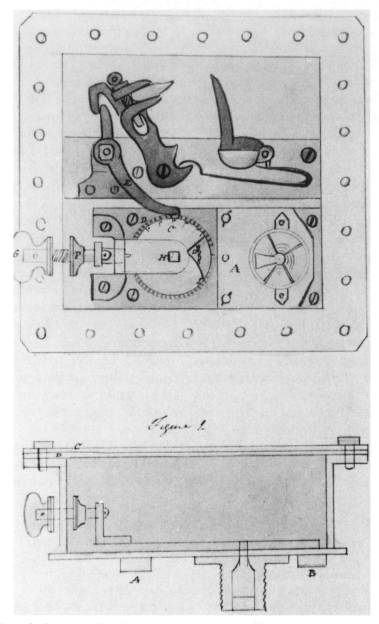

French drawing of Fulton's intricate clockwork mechanism for the mines used in his raid on Boulogne, 1806. Alofsen Collection, The New Jersey Historical Society, Alan Frazer, photographer

then ordered the cask to [be] thrown overboard. . . . I think
they must have heard the splashing of the casks from the
shore, as they commenced firing musketry immediately, the
balls coming over the boats. This was the first firing that
took place.[25]

Note that Allison's craft was a "long cutter," not a catamaran.
Another officer present described the weapons and the raid in
more detail. He noted that the containers "were filled with
combustibles, and covered with pitch about two inches thick."
He also said that, once the pin was removed, the timing device
was set for ten minutes. This indicates that some guess work
was involved regarding the speed of the tide and like matters.
The officer further stated:

> . . . No sooner had we approached near the shore, than
> the enemy spy'd us, and began to fire upon us from every
> quarter, when they saw the explosion of our machines. . . .
> Had one of the enemy's shells fallen on our ship, and set the
> *infernals* (as they are termed by the fleet) on fire, there
> would have been an end to us. I am happy to inform you
> there were no lives lost on our side; and we have some reason
> to think, the enemy sustained very little, if any injury, our
> machines not answering the purpose for which they were in-
> tended. We could perceive this morning some of them were
> driven on shore, without having either taken fire or ex-
> ploded, and unfortunately fell into the enemy's hands, some
> thousands of whom were assembled on the beach to look at
> them. We expect to . . . return the remainder of the ma-
> chines into store, from which, as a true friend to the service,
> I heartily wish we had never taken them.[26]

Lord Keith's assessment of the operation was more positive. He
felt that it was to be considered an experiment rather than a
major combat operation and advised the Admiralty: ". . . I
think it my duty to state to them my conviction, that in the
event of any great accumulation of the enemy's force in their
roadsteads, an extensive and combined operation of a similar
nature will hold forth a reasonable prospect of a successful
result."[27] Years later Fulton reflected that the selection of small
craft as delivery vehicles for the mines had been a good one. He

wrote, "While I was with the British blockading fleet off the coast of Boulogne in 1804 and 1805, I acquired some experience on the kind of rowboat best calculated for active movements . . . hence I propose clinker-built boats, each twenty-seven feet long. . . ."[28]

The performance of Fulton's mines at Boulogne demonstrated that the "New Curiosities" were still in their initial stages of development and had not yet been perfected. Damage to the French fleet was negligible, although the French commander did admit losing one craft. The so-called Catamaran Expedition, however, which had lasted seven hours, was significant in that it was an imaginative and extensive combat operation that caught the attention of many people in both England and France. Fulton's intricate timing mechanism, for instance, was an excellent example of the inventor's skill and craftsmanship. Even if the operational results were less than a total success, top British officials were not unhappy. The first lord of the Admiralty, Viscount Melville, said, "I would ask any candid man if in the course of his life he ever heard of so few failures in so extensive a night operation."[29] On the other hand, Sir Evan Nepean, Irish secretary and the former secretary of the Admiralty, warned of the pitfalls in this type of venture:

> If the plan which I am told has been resorted to should have been carried into execution with success, we may expect that the enemy will some time or another retaliate, and we shall have much more to lose than they have by such retaliation. In short, it appears to me if navies are to be destroyed by such means . . . our naval strength can no longer be counted on.[30]

In other words, Evan Nepean believed that Fulton's naval weapons would ultimately work against large naval powers such as Britain, as they could as easily destroy a large fleet as a small one. There would be others who would argue similarly against the use of Fulton's weapons. Fulton contended, however, that his weapons' tremendous power to destroy could make nations fearful of ever going to war. In particular, he

felt, the moored mine he was then developing for harbor defense would be a strong deterrent to a nautical invasion.

For the next few weeks, top officers in the Admiralty vigor-
ously debated the merits of Fulton's system. Lord Melville told
Keith to control those officers—one rear admiral in particular
—who were criticizing the venture. Melville indicates that
Lord Home Popham was actively involved in the controversy
when he writes, "I am well aware that Sir Home Popham is an
object of envy with some, of jealousy with others, but in pro-
portion as he is . . . run down, it is the duty of the Government
to run him up."[31]

Lords Melville and Keith next considered sending Fulton on
another expedition, this time further south against the port of
Rochefort on the Bay of Biscay. However, bad weather and the
approach of winter made them decide to postpone operations
until the next spring. Fulton was at Dover at this time requesting additional training for the crew that was to participate in
operations with his mines. In November, Melville received
news that supported his belief in Fulton's weapons and tactics.
The Admiralty chief wrote to Keith:

> . . . I have the satisfaction to tell you that by information
> from France which I have this morning received, the alarm
> created everywhere by the operations at Boulogne exceeded
> everything we have ever supposed. The pannick [sic] has
> been conveyed from Boulogne by the seamen and soldiers
> there to the other ports, particularly Brest, and the pannick
> has laid hold of the army intended for the invasion at every
> place from whence it was intended to come. It may require
> further consideration how far something should not be done
> to keep up and increase the pannick.[32]

Melville's comments indicate that Fulton's 1804 Catamaran
Expedition, through its psychological effect rather than
through actual damage to the enemy, may have played a much
more significant role in Napoleon's failure to invade England
than has heretofore been realized.

In the spring of 1805, Robert Fulton again prepared for action. Most of the French fleet had been temporarily shifted to
Cameret Bay off Brest. Fulton and the officers of the British

fleet were directed to be ready for another attack on the French "if a fair opportunity presents itself." On 13 May Fulton requested permission of Keith to blow up a wooden fort at Calais with a single mine filled with 1,500 pounds of powder. Fulton's plan was to send a small craft out on a moonless night "to run a carcass under the fort" in order to see "the effect of the perpendicular action of powder." Fulton added that the attack "may have a tendency to cheer the public mind," as "not one enterprise is in motion to cheer the hearts of Englishmen." Keith replied two days later that, although he felt that the destruction of a fort at Boulogne would be more detrimental to France than Fort Rouge at Calais, he would forward Fulton's request to the Admiralty. Nothing further was heard of this proposal.

Robert Fulton was becoming increasingly convinced that the government was stalling in giving him an opportunity to conduct experiments and operations with his mines. On 18 July 1805, he complained directly to William Pitt that he had written the government on several occasions without receiving an answer. This lack of response, Fulton said, indicated that the government did not intend to use his weapons further. He requested an answer and said that he looked forward to returning to the United States soon. Fulton sent an even more bellicose letter to Pitt the following month, requesting "a small squadron of three frigates, and one or two cutters to carry boats, catamarans, carcases [sic], and implements. . . ." This mission was to be commanded by "an active, enterprising officer" with an open authorization to cruise and attack any enemy ship. Fulton also posed a question to Pitt that could be interpreted as a veiled threat, in case his plan should not be adopted, "Is it the best policy of the British Government to make it my interest to let it rest in its present state?"[33] In other words, Fulton was saying that he realized the English wanted his naval weapons not so much to use them as to keep the French from employing them. So be it, Fulton reasoned, but the English were still going to have to pay for them.

Fulton's pressure on Pitt had some effect, at least temporarily. On 10 September, Lord Castlereagh wrote to Lord Barham, the new first lord of the Admiralty, requesting him to take Fulton's weapons out of storage at Portsmouth, and ready them for operations. Barham had replaced Melville as naval chief. Melville was in serious trouble, having been charged with financial irregularities in Pitt's previous administration. He was later impeached, and, although acquitted, never recovered his former influence. This was particularly unfortunate for Fulton, as Melville had generally been sympathetic to his naval warfare schemes. As Barham was not as effectual in his post, the new and energetic war secretary, Robert Stewart, Viscount Castlereagh, played an increasingly important role in the Fulton negotiations from 1805 on. There are two extreme views of Castlereagh. His future diplomatic achievements in the conception and development of the "Concert of Europe" following the Congress of Vienna in 1814, and his conciliatory relations with America have resulted in most favorable assessments by modern scholars. On the other hand, Castlereagh's domestic and Irish policies would so alienate some of his countrymen that the poet Percy Bysshe Shelley would write in "The Masque of Anarchy":

> I met Murder on his way,
> He had a mask like Castlereagh.

One day in 1822, worn out from overwork, Castlereagh would go home, pick up a razor from his dressing table, and slit his throat.

Back in London in September of 1805, Castlereagh told the naval operational commander, now Sir Sidney Smith, of the new mission proposed for Fulton and his naval weapons. The target was again to be the French fleet at Boulogne, almost a year to the day later. Castlereagh asked Smith to consider Fulton's most recent request for "9 row galleys, at 12 men each" and "10 catamarans, at 2 men each," for the assault, which presumably were delivered to the inventor.[34]

Sir Sidney Smith and his naval force were stationed off Boulogne late in September. The attack began there shortly after midnight on 1 October 1805. As in the 1804 Catamaran Expedition, Fulton's mines were to be dispatched two at a time, each attached to opposite ends of the same line, a delivery technique that Fulton had continued to practice over the past year. The French referred to these connected mines as "chains of fireships."

Rear Admiral La Crosse, commander in chief of the French fleet at Boulogne, stated that "a warm firing" began shortly after midnight, following which one of his ships was "surrounded by a chain of Fire-ships conducted by several pinnaces." His men succeeded in cutting the chain, but "one of the Fire-ships having exploded near the (French) Gun-boat, she was thrown up and covered with water, and had no other damage than her windows broken and some shot aboard." Reporting that the attack ceased at two in the morning with no fatal casualties, La Crosse did admit that four French sailors were killed at daybreak when one of the "infernal machines" they were towing up the beach exploded. His men also found "several wrecks of the Fire-ships" on the beach, as well as "a lock like that of the Fire-machines which the English used last year with as much ridicule and as little success."[35] Napoleon did not miss a chance to point out the expense and ineffectiveness of this raid, sarcastically describing it as "breaking the windows of the good citizens of Boulogne with English guineas."[36]

Rather surprisingly, Robert Fulton's assessment of the 1805 Boulogne raid does not differ too much from the French account. He wrote:

> Captain Siccombe, in a galley with eight men and his coxswain, placed two torpedoes . . . between the buoy and cable of a French gun-brig, in Boulogne roads. The tide drove them until they both lay perpendicular to her sides. When the French saw Captain Siccombe advancing without answering the countersign, they exclaimed that the infernal machines were coming, and fired a volley of musketry at his boat, but without touching a man. The moment the French fired, fearing the effect of the explosions, they all ran aft, and were in the greatest confusion. . . .[37]

Fulton also said that Siccombe's crew killed four of the enemy with small arms fire, which differed from La Crosse's report of

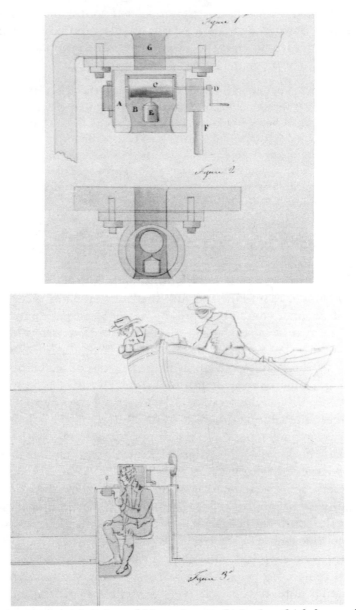

Robert Fulton drawing of his cork-note device by which he would send messages from his submerged submarine to the surface, 1806. Alofsen Collection, The New Jersey Historical Society, Alan Frazer, photographer

no casualties. The usually supremely self-confident inventor, however, downgraded his weapons in his report, admitting that they failed to sink the target. He also downplayed the scope and nature of the raid, describing it as:

> . . . an experiment on a small scale to try the effect of 4 of my Submarine bombs or *Torpedoes*. They were carried in by two small boats which the french have magnified to many fire ships with a formidable attack of boats which shews that they were much frightened or that the public must be amused with a long story. however the *Torpedoes* did not produce the desired effect, and I saw a great prejudice arise in the minds of the officers against them. . . .[38]

One can probably best assess the 1 October 1805 Boulogne raid by taking into account equally both the French and Fulton's versions of it.

Fulton's report had noted that although both his mines had exploded, they had failed to sink the ship. He later theorized that his copper containers were too heavy to be positioned effectively against the target ship. In other words, as below water the hull of a ship curves inward towards its keel, the mines were being set too deep to rub up against the sides of the ship. Attaching a pine box filled with cork to each mine, Fulton believed, would give his weapons the buoyancy they needed.

Eager to test his new modification, Fulton moved quickly in an effort to quell mounting criticism of his weapons. With government backing, he procured a Danish brig, the *Dorothea*, and anchored her in Walmer Roads, off Pitt's country estate, Walmer Castle, near Dover. Fulton hoped to blow the brig up in full view of most of the top leaders of the government. He spent the fourteenth of October practicing with the crew, and on the following day the test took place. Many naval officers present were skeptical. One Captain Owen remarked that he would remain on board the *Dorothea* during the test, and a Captain Kingston said that if a "torpedo" was to be set off under his cabin while he was seated at dinner, "he should feel no concern for the consequence." Not too surprisingly, however, the brig was deserted when the test began.[39]

In mid-afternoon of 15 October 1805, Robert Fulton gave
the signal for the run on the *Dorothea* to begin. Two boats,
each manned with eight men, under the command of a Lieutenant Robinson, comprised the naval contingent. One galley
in particular, according to Fulton, "rushed forward and grap-
pled the *Torpedo* line in the cable of the brig." Fulton was
again using the "chain" technique of attaching two mines to a
line and directing this at the target ship's anchor. However,
this time his mines were kept buoyant by the cork-filled boxes.
The clock mechanism was set for fifteen minutes (Fulton later
said eighteen) and at the appointed time, in Fulton's words:
". . . the awful explosion took place; it lifted the whole body of
the Vessel almost out of the water and broke her completely in

*On 15 October 1805, Robert Fulton successfully blew up the brig
the* Dorothea, *the first man in history to sink a large ship with a
mine.* **American State Papers, Naval Affairs**

two in the middle. The main mast and pumps were blown out of her and in one minuet [*sic*] nothing of her was to be seen but floating fragments. . . ."[40] Although Pitt suddenly had to return to London and thus missed the demonstration, Fulton was exultant. With the problem of buoyancy corrected, the American wrote, "All doubts are now removed on the power and simplicity of this Invention."[41] This was the high point of Robert Fulton's work in naval warfare in England. He was the first man in history to sink a large ship with a mine.

Fulton's good fortune continued as the government now advanced him a large sum of money. Castlereagh wrote to the first lord of the Admiralty:

> Although the precise conditions on which the full Reward depends, have not yet been fulfilled by the actual destruction of an Enemy's ship, the application and powers of this system have been proved so far by actual experiment, as to have entitled the Inventor in the judgment of the Chancellor of the Exchequer, and of the late First Lord of the Admiralty to an advance of one Quarter of the sum promised, viz 10,000 pounds.[42]

Fulton's following letter to his sister Betsy, written on the same day that Castlereagh arranged the monetary advance, reflects his feelings of triumph. In it Fulton reminisces with his sister about an episode when he was twelve years old:

> . . . You and Bill had turned me and the cat out of the truckle bed. It was a winter's evening about eight o'clock. I instantly flew to the tongs, and as I stood in my shirt with uplifted arms ready to knock all your brains out, you were much astonished at my resolute manner and wickedness . . . that you began to cry, and said you were sure I should some day be hanged. The tears of a woman have always affected me, and they did so then. I was instantly disarmed, and, throwing down the tongs, I went to you, took you by the hand, and said, "No, Betsy, I shall live to be the protector of you and the family," and I am now very happy to have it in my power to verify what I then asserted.[43]

Fulton's euphoric state lasted approximately two weeks. It

looked for awhile as if he were going to get another chance to test his weapons in combat. His mines as well as Congreve's rockets were scheduled by Cartwright to be used by the Royal Navy against the French forces at Cadiz. On 27 October, Castlereagh wrote to the naval commander there, Lord Nelson:

> . . . I have not thought it desirable to send either Mr. Congreve or Mr. Francis to your lordship, till they have provided themselves with all the necessary means of giving effect to the respective modes of attack. Since your lordship sailed, the power of Mr. Francis's instrument have been satisfactorily ascertained by an experiment upon a large vessel purchased for that purpose. . . . I hope to forward both these weapons soon to your lordship, and I am sure your lordship will facilitate their application.[44]

Castlereagh's letter was, unfortunately, six days too late. 21 October 1805 is one of those key dates that "every English schoolboy knows," according to the mid-nineteenth century British historian Macauley, for it is the date of Admiral Horatio Nelson's heroic victory over the French and death at the battle of Trafalgar. With this annihilation of the French fleet, the British no longer needed Fulton's weapons. Earl St. Vincent put the matter very succinctly to Fulton when he told him that "Pitt was the greatest fool that ever existed, to encourage a mode of war which they who commanded the seas did not want, and which, if successful, would deprive them of it."[45]

With the vision of the *Dorothea* exploding before his eyes, as he once reportedly said, "like a shattered egg shell," Fulton's conscience began to bother him. The day after the explosion, he wrote, "one reflection which gives me some pain that In vessels thus attacked it will be impossible to save the men — and many a worthy character must perish . . ."[46] Five years later he would rationalize this problem:

> . . . men, without reflecting . . . exclaim that it is barbarous to blow up a ship with all her crew. This I admit, and lament that it should be necessary; but all wars are barbarous, and particularly wars of offence. It is barbarous for a

ship of war to fire into a peaceable merchant vessel, kill part
of her people, take her and the property, and reduce the
proprietor . . . to penury. It was barbarous to bombard Co-
penhagen, set fire to the city, and destroy innocent women
and children. It would be barbarous for ships of war to enter
the harbor of New York, fire on the city, destroy property,
and murder many of the peaceable inhabitants; yet we have
great reason to expect such a scene of barbarism and dis-
tress, unless means are taken to prevent it; therefore, if torpedoes should prevent such acts of violence, the invention
must be humane.[47]

Many British officers could not reason as Fulton did. One officer who had participated in the 1805 Boulogne raid
declaimed:

This species of warfare, unmanly, and I may say assassin-
like, I always abhorred. Under cover of the night, to glide
with muffled oars beneath the bows of a vessel, and when
her crew is least suspicious of impending danger, to affix
such an infernal machine beneath her bottom, and in a moment hurl them to destruction, in what does it differ from
the midnight attack of the burglar, who steals into your
house, and robs his sleeping victim at once of money and
life?[48]

Admiral George Berkeley, the British naval commander in
America whose orders that American ships be searched for
British deserters later resulted in the unnecessary *Chesapeake–
Leopard* incident of 1807, wrote:

The Author or rather projector of your Torpedos [*sic*]
tried his hand upon John Bull's credulity . . . and after a
very expensive Trial the scheme was scouted not perhaps so
much from its Failure, as from the Baseness & Cowardice of
this species of Warfare. All stratagems are however allowed
in War, and there are certain Regulations attached to Ingen-
uity of this kind which I rather suspect Mr. Fulton is not acquainted with, at least in England he rather *Blinked* the
Question. Every Projector ought to be the Man, who first
makes trial of his own Device, and then he is entitled to the
Reward of his Merit. An officer who commands a Fire Ship,

has a gold chain round his Neck, if he is successful, But if he
is taken, a Hempen One is the premium he is sure to Receive, which I think Friend Fulton would rather be surprised
at. . . .[49]

Even some of Fulton's strongest English supporters lost their
zeal after Trafalgar. Senior naval officer Sir Sidney Smith complained to Castlereagh on 22 November:

> . . . Mr. Francis's coffers, we know, will blow *brigs up,*
> and may larger ships, but the placing them is a perilous bus-
> iness; his boats are too ticklish for these seas: all have come
> on board full of water, and kept up by the cork only; but
> the men wet and discouraged by risk and suffering. This cli-
> mate, at this season, will not do for these things. . . .[50]

Fulton began to feel that his naval weapons would receive no
further support in England. He told Castlereagh, "as to myself,
having shown how to construct the carcasses, and apply them
with simplicity and certainty, little more can be required of
me."[51] Fulton continued to propose grandiose naval schemes to
Sir Sidney Smith and others, but he seems to have lost his enthusiasm. On 13 December 1805, Fulton sent a terse letter to
Castlereagh asking for a final settlement. The British government no longer seemed disposed favorably towards him. The
American envoy in London, James Monroe, advised Secretary
of State James Madison in December that British officials "had
apprehended of improper views and designs being entertained
against this country by Mr. Barlow and Mr. Fulton. . . ."[52]
While Monroe does not elaborate on his statement, it may be
that the British were upset over Fulton's and Barlow's well-
known republican proclivities. The breakdown in relations between the United States and Britain that would culminate in
the War of 1812 was just beginning.

On 6 January 1806, Robert Fulton officially registered his
complaints with William Pitt and requested a settlement. He
wrote:

> Lord Melville was very friendly to my enterprise. . . .
> Since his leaving the Admiralty I have waited from month to
> month, hoping Lord Barham would follow Lord Melville's

measures, but I have reason to believe he disapproves of the whole plan or is indifferent to it. . . . The submarine mode of warfare must be organized to render it efficient or I must abandon it. . . . I do not at present see that I can be of any further material service in this system of warfare; I therefore propose as the most equitable arrangement between his Majesty's Ministers and me, to revert to the principle which brought me to this country and finally settle with them.[53]

For his settlement Fulton requested: 10,000 pounds "for leaving France and coming to England"; 100,000 pounds for "clearly demonstrating that ships of war can be destroyed by my engines with more ease and less risque than by any method now in practice"; and, most audaciously, his present annual salary of 2,400 pounds for life and 60,000 pounds to ensure that he would "remain tranquil." Fulton even had the nerve to clearly explain the purpose of these payments—so "I should not exercise or be the cause of exercising my invention against the fleets of great Britain." In a masterpiece of understatement, Fulton told Pitt, "You will no doubt at first thought consider my demand great. . . ."[54]

The effect of all this on William Pitt is not known as he died two weeks later, probably more broken by Napoleon's victory at Austerlitz than by Fulton's grossly excessive financial demands.

Robert Fulton also had some stunning news for his friends the Barlows. He wrote his friend, now back in America, that he planned to marry a rich English lady, presumably a widow with several children. Barlow was horrified. Decrying his friend's decision, he wrote ironically, "What is perhaps more unfortunate for you, she has a fortune [which] renders it extremely improbable that she can be happy in this country."[55] Barlow also stressed the fact that Fulton was an American who had been away from his country too long. He should forget the lady and come home. Fulton would later take Barlow's advice.

In response to Fulton's request for a final financial settlement, Pitt's successors agreed to some sort of settlement in principle but felt the exact amount should be decided by an ar-

bitration board. The primary British official now dealing with
Fulton in 1806 was the new first lord of the Admiralty, Lord
Howick, later better known as Earl Grey. While having little
love for any American, he particularly disliked Jeffersonians
like Fulton. This thought could not have been very comforting
to the American inventor.

During the next few months Fulton wrote scores of letters to
various members of the new Grenville ministry, of which Grey
was a member. Fulton's letters were increasingly belligerent in
tone and cannot have helped his case much.

Finally, the arbitration board, composed of Sir Charles
Blagden, Thomas Hamilton, Alexander Davison, and Fulton's
old friend, Edmund Cartwright, duly convened. After meeting
in session for some time, they announced on 5 August 1806
that "the plan of the said Robert Fulton is not so far novel,
practicable, and effective as to entitle him" to the terms of the
original contract, let alone Fulton's grandiose demands of 6
January. The board awarded him what amounted to what he
had already been paid, 14,000 pounds, plus salary and inci-
dentals due him in the amount of 1,640 pounds.[56]

Disgusted, because his threat to divulge his secrets had no effect on the British, Fulton took his pittance and prepared to
depart for America. Even after he booked passage, he made
one final attempt to persuade Grenville to change his mind, to
no avail.

Many, if not most, men might grow exceedingly bitter after
pursuing a goal for many years and finding nothing in the
main but frustration and disappointment. Not so with Robert
Fulton. One of his most attractive personal attributes was his
ability to maintain his good spirits, enthusiasm, and optimism
in spite of the harshest adversity. As the departure date grew
closer for his return to the United States, the country to which
he had always been faithful, and which he had not seen in
twenty years, one could almost feel his exuberance heighten.
His last letter from Europe was written, as might be expected,
to his great friend Barlow: "I am now busy winding up everything, and will leave London about the 23rd for Falmouth,

from whence I shall sail in the packet the first week in October, and be with you, I hope, in November, perhaps about the 14th, my birthday—so you must have a roast goose ready!"[57] So Robert Fulton departed Europe, on his way to a date with a roast goose, to his greatest fame with a steamboat voyage on the Hudson in less than a year, and to further work in the field of naval warfare.

4

Homecoming,
1807–1814

Following his return to the United States from England, Robert Fulton would continue to work on his mines, this time attempting to interest his own government in his weapons. During these years, he would conduct two major "torpedo" tests using target vessels in New York Harbor, experiment with several new nautical devices, and engage in diverse naval activities against the British during the War of 1812.

Fulton's ship arrived in New York on 13 December 1806. He had always remained steadfastly loyal to the United States, and the depth of his emotions upon returning to his native land after an absence of twenty years may be imagined. Reports of his growing fame had preceded him, and it is noteworthy that one eastern newspaper's announcement of Fulton's return did not specifically mention the steamboat, but singled out instead his work in the area of naval warfare: ". . . His return will be an important acquisition to our country in the various branches of public improvement . . . and we cannot but hope that his system of *submarine navigation* may be advantageously united with that of our *gun boats,* to form the cheapest and surest defence of our harbors and coasts."[1]

Fulton's first concern was to contact his mentor, Joel Barlow, who was temporarily lodged in Philadelphia. The two friends met there and consulted about the publication of the expensive American edition of Barlow's *Columbiad* for which Fulton had prepared a portfolio of elaborate historical illustrations.

Barlow invited Fulton for an extended stay at his new estate in Washington. The poet proudly described his new home:

> I have here a most delightful situation. . . . It is a
> beautiful hill, about one mile from the Potomac . . . with
> Washington and Georgetown under my eye. . . . If you have
> a plan of the city I can show you the very spot. Look at the
> stream called Rock Creek, that divides Washington and
> Georgetown. . . . My hill is that white, circular spot. I find
> the name of Belair has been already given to many places in
> Maryland and Virginia, so by the advice of friends, we have
> changed it for one that is quite new—Calorama [sic] from
> the Greek, signifying "fine view," and this place represents
> one of the finest views in America.[2]

During his sojourn at Kalorama, Robert Fulton pursued a wide variety of activities. He designed a summer house for the Barlows, tested a steamboat model on Rock Creek near their estate, and demonstrated his "torpedo" at Kalorama to important government officials. When the P Street bridge over Rock Creek was opened in 1935, the District of Columbia commissioners considered a motion to name it "Robert Fulton Bridge" because of his nautical activities in the area.[3]

In January 1807, Fulton and Barlow attended a testimonial dinner in Washington for Meriwether Lewis, recently returned from his momentous exploration of the continent with William Clark. Barlow composed an extended poem in honor of Lewis, and Fulton offered this nationalistic toast: "The American Eagle—When she expands her wings from the Atlantic to the Pacific Ocean, may she quench her thunders in both."[4] Robert Fulton found that, almost effortlessly, he was moving in much grander social and political circles than he had been before departing from America twenty years earlier. Many of his new friends were Jeffersonian Republicans, and their influence proved to be very useful to him as he planned his first major demonstration of "torpedo" warfare in the United States.

Robert Fulton soon returned to New York, where he worked on his Hudson River steamboat and prepared for his "torpedo" test. On 22 June 1807, the *Chesapeake–Leopard* affair stunned the nation (described earlier in this book in the "War of 1807"). When the immediate threat of war had passed, Fulton scheduled his New York "torpedo" test for 20 July 1807. Prior to this, however, he invited local dignitaries to Governors Island in New York Bay for a close-up view and lecture on the efficacy of his naval weapon. A large crowd gathered about Fulton as he dramatically announced: "Gentlemen, this is a charged torpedo, with which precisely in its present state, I mean to blow up a vessel; it contains one hundred and seventy pounds of gunpowder, and if I were to suffer the clockwork to run fifteen minutes, I have no doubt that it would blow this fortification to atoms."[5] It was noted that the crowd thinned considerably upon hearing Fulton's words, and that he somewhat amusedly commented that fear often arises out of ignorance.

Fulton planned to have a run made on an anchored target ship, much in the same way that the *Dorothea* had been successfully attacked in 1805 in England. On the afternoon of the scheduled day, the first run was made against the 200-ton brig

Swedish replica of Robert Fulton's mine, loaned to the Navy Memorial Museum, Washington Navy Yard, by the Marin-Museum, Karlskrona, Sweden

serving as the target ship. Two connected "torpedoes" were thrown into the water, and the line engaged the ship's anchor cable, but the mine failed to explode. Fulton discovered that he had placed the firing mechanism in such a way as to cause the powder to fall out of its pans. After adjusting the mechanism, he made a second attempt. This time the "torpedoes" missed the ship and exploded approximately 100 yards away, shooting a great column of water high in the air. The third run was successful. A newspaper report of 21 July stated: "The experiment of Mr. Fulton for blowing up ships of war was made about 7 o'clock yesterday afternoon upon a brig of 200 tons burthen, and succeeded to the utmost wishes of the inventor. When the machinery had taken effect, the brig's foremast was thrown up several feet, and in less than a minute she totally disappeared."[6] Fulton was ebullient. He exulted, "She was rent in two, and went to the bottom in 20 seconds."[7] In a more detailed later account, Fulton stated that approximately 2,000 persons had witnessed the event, that "the effect and result" were "much the same as the Dorothea," and that "the practicability of destroying vessels by this means has been fully proved."[8]

On 28 July 1807, Robert Fulton wrote a lengthy report of the experiment to President Jefferson. After describing the test, he dwelt at some length on his plans for further development of "torpedo" warfare. Fulton stated that he had found after much experimentation two primary ways of using his "torpedoes." The first way, to be employed only against enemy vessels at anchor, involved connecting the torpedoes "by a line and chain 100 feet long," and placing them eight to ten feet below the surface of the water, so as to be invisible to the enemy. Each mine would be suspended from a cork float. The two mines would be connected by the chain, the two main floats by the line, and then several other floats would be placed on the surface in between to hold the chain up. Fulton's system had grown more elaborate since the attack at Boulogne.

Fulton had also devised a means of attack against vessels underway that differed radically from the method used against stationary targets. He proposed to use an eighteen-inch-long harpoon gun, placed in the bow of a large rowboat, to fire a "single bolt of Iron two feet long with an eye and barbed point" into the wooden hull of a moving ship. A sixty-foot line would be connected to the eye of the harpoon on one end, and to a mine on the other. Fulton told the president that he had experimented with this system at a distance of forty feet from the target and had driven the harpoon in "6 inches deep." The "clock" for detonating the charge, he said, should be set at two

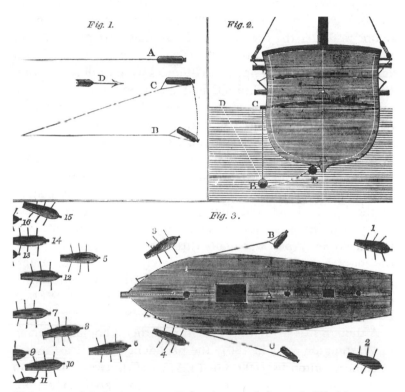

Figure 1 and 2 demonstrate Fulton's use of the cork-filled box to insure that the mine makes contact with the target ship. A = Unattached mine; B = mine attached to C, the cork-filled box. Figure 3 illustrates the multi-boat attack pattern to circumvent the target ship's evasive action. Reprinted from Torpedo War and Submarine Explosions, *Plate V*

minutes. This time should be too short for the enemy to find means to prevent the explosion but long enough to allow the boat crew to withdraw safely. Foreseeing that the enemy vessel could avoid the contact and explosion by turning the ship and causing the mine to swing free, the inventor proposed a large-scale attack. Twenty boats with one "torpedo" each would attack the vessel, ten on each side. Thus, no matter which way the target vessel turned, she could not escape from all of the mines.

Fulton concluded his letter to Jefferson with an appeal that the U.S. Navy systematize his "torpedo" tactics. With an attempt to flatter the president and emphasize the economy of his weapons, Fulton wrote: ". . . your capacious mind will readily trace all the happy consequences which will result from the success and general practice of this invention. . . . is there any mode of defence so cheap so easy of practice so fitted to common understanding?"[9] Fulton was appealing to Jefferson's well-known aversion to large and expensive navies. As far as large-scale naval construction is concerned, Jefferson's administration has been described as the worst in American history. Jefferson favored small, inexpensive gunboats over large ships of the line and believed that the nation could best achieve peace by limiting the navy and not taking part in an arms race in peacetime. When war really threatened, the president felt, the country could then build a completely new naval force. Jefferson's general views did not seem in accord with the tumultuous atmosphere of 1807, but they did correspond to Robert Fulton's ideas.

Although it is likely that Fulton first met Thomas Jefferson in Washington early in 1807, the president was at least aware of Robert Fulton by 1800. On 13 April of that year, Jefferson stated he owned a copy of Fulton's treatise on canal navigation. During the following year, Joel Barlow wrote Jefferson of Fulton's work in naval warfare, telling him among other things that Fulton "hopes very soon to demonstrate the practicability of destroying military navies altogether."[10] Although Fulton's meaning is not known, upon his arrival in England from

France, he wrote to Jefferson that some of the president's letters had been "committed to my care in Paris."[11]

On 16 August 1807, Jefferson responded to Fulton's extended report of 28 July. The president's tone was very
supportive:

> Your letter of July 28 came to hand just as I was leaving
> Washington. It has not sooner been in my power to acknowl-
> edge it. I consider your Torpedoes as very valuable means of
> the defence of harbours, & I have no doubt we should adopt
> them to a considerable degree, not that I go the whole
> length (as I believe you do) of considering them as solely to
> be relied on. . . . [12]

Jefferson was concerned that the enemy could find means to
protect their ships from the mines. In particular, the mines
used against moored vessels, he felt, would be relatively easy to
parry. The president then wrote, "I have ever looked to the
submarine boat as most to be depended on for attaching them
[mines], and though I see no mention of it in your letter . . . I
am in hopes it is not abandoned as impracticable. I should
wish to see a corps of young men trained to this service."[13] The
president asked for further information on Fulton's submarine
and said that he would write the Navy Department about the
inventor's proposals. When he did so four days later, the president again stressed the "submarine boat" rather than mines.
Referring to his vision of young men specifically trained to be
submariners, Jefferson believed that "the very name of a corps
of submarine engineers would be a defence."[14] Unfortunately
for the development of the submarine, Fulton did not respond
to this presidential request for further comments on the submarine, having lost interest in that project. Also, Jefferson had
delayed too long in responding to Fulton. The day after the
president dispatched his letter, the inventor had commenced
his historic voyage up the Hudson in his steamboat.

The Boulton and Watt low-pressure engine that Fulton had
ordered while in England had probably arrived in the United
States before Robert Fulton did, as the English had finally

granted a license to export it on 22 March 1805. Early in March 1807, Fulton and Robert Livingston revived their partnership by clarifying their financial responsibilities in an agreement signed at Livingston's estate by the Hudson called "Clermont." A Charles Brownne was contracted to construct the steamboat at his New York shipyard, but the concept, the mathematical calculations, and the successful combination of a low-pressure engine, side paddlewheels, and hull design were Robert Fulton's. As the day of the trial run approached, New York newspapers were strangely silent. There was no mention of the craft on the day of departure for Albany, 17 August, but Catherine Mitchill, the wife of the noted scientist Samuel L. Mitchill, did observe the occasion. She wrote, "Mr. Fulton has gone to Albany with his steamboat. He is a curious looking thing and I expect he will frighten some of the old Dutch men half out of their wits. They will conclude the enemy is coming in earnest with a machine to blow them all up."[15] The New York newspapers were dominated by stories of the trial of Aaron Burr, who had been arrested for treason after allegedly attempting to set up a new republic in the Southwest, and they did not acknowledge the historic voyage until 22 August. A controversy has arisen in recent years over the name of Fulton's first American steamboat. One authority notes that the vessel's official name was *North River Steam Boat*. A second scholar believes that the vessel should be called simply *Steam Boat*, because that was the name that Fulton preferred. What is significant is that neither scholar favors "Clermont," the name taught to millions of young Americans by well-intentioned but misinformed schoolteachers.[16] Fulton described this first voyage in an extensive letter to Joel Barlow. Significantly, he concluded this letter by saying, "I will not admit that it is half so important as the torpedo system of defence and attack."[17]

On the afternoon of 18 August, as the steamboat pulled into the Livingston estate landing, Chancellor Livingston called for silence and announced the engagement of his distant cousin Harriet Livingston to Robert Fulton. The forty-two-year-old inventor had met Harriet, roughly half his age, some weeks earlier for the first time.* Within the same twenty-four hours, Fulton had reached the heights of both professional and personal happiness. Interestingly, the chancellor did not make the engagement announcement until after the steamboat had been proved successful.[18] Robert Fulton and Harriet Livingston were married on 7 January 1808. Although Ruth Barlow was not happy with Fulton's marriage, the inventor's old painting master was exultant. Benjamin West wrote from London: " . . . It gave Mrs. West and me so much gratification to find from you, that you had become a married man to a most amiable Lady of the city of New York. . . . I congratulate you on that event, as it was always my wish you should form such an interest in your native country by marriage as to give you permanency there. . . . "[19] Robert and Harriet Fulton settled in lower Manhattan and eventually had four children, all born in succeeding years.

Robert Fulton was busily engaged in his steamboat operations for several weeks. His instructions to the steamboat's skipper, a Captain Brink, reveal Fulton's attitude towards shipboard discipline and the ultimate responsibility of the ship's commander. Fulton ordered:

> You must insist on each one doing his duty, or turn him on shore and put another in his place. Every thing must be kept in order—every thing in its place, and all parts of the boat scoured and clean. It is not sufficient to tell men to do a thing, but stand over them and make them do it. One pair of good and quick eyes is worth six pair of hands in a commander. If the boat is dirty or out of order, the fault should be yours. Let no man be idle when there is the least thing to do, and make them move quickly.[20]

---

*It might be noted in passing that the Robert Fulton story was last told by Hollywood in a 1940 Darryl F. Zanuck-produced film entitled "Little Old New York." When Fulton was introduced in the film to his future bride, the filmmakers had the audacity to have him say, "Miss Livingston, I presume"? Fulton was played in the film by the British actor Richard Greene, while the better-known American actor Fred MacMurray had the lesser role of Charles Brownne, the boatbuilder. Brenda Joyce played Harriet. No one mentioned naval warfare!

In December 1807, Robert Fulton wrote to Jefferson again about tactics for making large-scale attacks with his mines. Instead of his previous plan to use twenty attack boats, however, Fulton now said that two "6 oar'd boats or galleys" would be sufficient, each boat to hold three "copper cases" and a crew of ten to handle them. He made no mention of the submarine as Jefferson had requested.[21]

Very shortly after he renewed his correspondence with the president, Fulton departed Washington with Barlow for a trip to the north. On the ninth of December, they each wrote to Jefferson on a variety of subjects. Fulton forwarded the president a tract of canals, and also played a little politics with the egalitarian Republican president, whose party was generally perceived as the political organ of democracy, while the Federalist party basically reflected the views of the privileged. Wrote Fulton, "I have struck at the arguments of the Aristocrats and Federalists of our country, and those feble [sic] or wavering minds devoid of philosophic reflection. . . . "[22] Barlow, in his letter of the same date to the president, wrote:

> . . . I have read the memoir of our friend Fulton I think it a real good thing. If this man is supported he will give us the liberty of the seas and a system of interior public improvements superior to what has been seen in any country. His whole soul is in these two subjects, as I had mentioned to you before his return to this country, and his energy is equal to the task. . . . [23]

How revealing that Robert Fulton cared much more deeply for canals and naval warfare than he did for the steamboat! Barlow wanted to add a pet project of his own, a "national institution," such as a museum for scientific display or a national university to complement Fulton's ideas. Jefferson politely acknowledged Fulton's letter, but wrote with more feeling to Barlow, "I doubt whether precedence will be given to your part of the plan before Mr. Fulton's. People generally have more feeling for canals & evade education."[24]

In order to demonstrate the efficiency of his weapons to members of Congress, Robert Fulton wanted to conduct a "torpedo" demonstration in Washington in 1808. Presumably this was to consist of displaying small models of his weapons. However, he became increasingly frustrated in his dealings with Jefferson's Secretary of the Navy Robert Smith. Although Smith had been born in Fulton's home town of Lancaster in 1757, this common origin did not help the inventor. Ironically, in 1800 Jefferson had first offered the naval secretaryship to Robert Livingston, soon to become Fulton's steamboat partner. After Livingston's refusal, Jefferson offered the post to Smith. Secretary Smith would not authorize any funds for Fulton's "torpedo" project. Fulton then asked him to release just two workmen from the naval department to work on the weapon, and Fulton would pay their wages. Smith refused. In despair, Fulton went directly to Jefferson for aid. In a letter to the president, Fulton voiced his long-time resentment against the naval establishment:

> Considering that in france [sic] and in England the whole
> opposition I met with was from gentlemen of the marine,
> and Knowing that they are hostile to my plan here my feel-
> ings are naturally alive to every coldness and procrastination
> I may meet with. But it is not to the *genius*, good judgment,
> Talents, Spirit, or broad thinking of any part of our marine
> that I look for . . . aid. . . . as far as I have seen they in
> talents do not surpass the common standerd [sic] of Mankind
> and never will throw new lights on the world. . . . [25]

Jefferson responded to Fulton's plea and gently ordered Smith to release the two workmen at government expense.[26] Advising Fulton of what he had done, the president put in a word of defence for Smith's actions. On 15 August 1808 he wrote Fulton, "You are sensible, too, that harassed as the offices are daily by the visions of unsound heads, even those solid inventions destined to better our condition, feel the effect of being grouped with them."[27] Jefferson had a point. Unlike the Navy Department today, the entire organization throughout most of Jefferson's administration was run by Secretary Smith with the help of only three clerks.

On 24 January 1809, Fulton wrote to Jefferson and requested

his support for a new "torpedo" experiment.[28] This was his last correspondence with Jefferson as president on the subject of naval warfare as James Madison had won the election of 1808 and was preparing to take office. Fulton lost no time in contacting the chief executive-to-be. After praising Madison, probably overmuch, he then proposed that Joel Barlow be appointed Madison's secretary of state. Strangely, Fulton's major reason for recommending his friend was not Barlow's experience in foreign affairs, but rather so that Barlow would be in a position to observe American politics from within the government in order to write a definitive history of the country.[29]

Before receiving Madison's answer, Fulton enthusiastically invited him to a harpoon demonstration at Kalorama during the middle of February 1809. Fulton indicated that he would be happy to go over his entire "torpedo" system with the president-elect at that time.[30] The inventor also invited Jefferson, as well as key members of Congress. Both Madison and Jefferson attended the demonstration, and Fulton felt that his experiments had made a favorable impression. A few days later he wrote a very frank letter to Madison in which he again complained about the naval establishment's opposition to his "torpedo" system. Fulton pointed out:

> . . . it needs but little penetration to discover that the gentlemen of the marine at Washington are not favorable to it. I excuse them as I would a Pope who rejected a profession of faith which might destroy his infalibility. [*sic*] But the nation and your future fame have a high interest in the success of Torpedo attack, And it might happen that the marine could be so directed as to powerfully aid in proving its Utility and if proved useful introduce it into practice.[31]

By this time Fulton had become aware that his friend Barlow had been rejected for the post of secretary of state. Ironically, Madison had appointed Jefferson's naval department head Robert Smith as his new secretary of state. Fulton, however, rarely stopped pursuing an idea until the person with whom he was dealing was overwhelmed by his own peculiar combination of audacity and honesty. Accordingly, the inventor now recommended that Madison appoint Joel Barlow as secretary of the Navy! Wrote Fulton:

> . . . Mr. Barlow could act as secretary of the Marine for only one year or 18 months. I think I can promise you a complete defence of our coast and harbors without either marine or fortifications. And in so doing I hope exhibit a mode of War which will give liberty to the seas. Mr. Barlow does not desire the situation *should it be Vacant* for any other reason than to promote a system which he conceives of the first importance. And with that View would willingly act as your friend and mine for a limited time. . . . [32]

Madison's feelings on receipt of this letter are not known, but might be imagined. Needless to say, Barlow did not get this appointment either. It went instead to Paul Hamilton, a planter from South Carolina. Hamilton was a rather unimaginative, mediocre man who has been judged harshly by history. His drinking problem increasingly contributed to his administration's lack of achievement, and he finally quietly resigned in December 1812.[33]

Throughout the remainder of 1809, Robert Fulton divided his time between the development of new steamboats and the planning of another, more elaborate "torpedo" experiment. Joel Barlow, as always, continued to support him. On the fourth of July that year, Barlow made a major address to the public in Washington. He concluded his orderly and well-structured patriotic speech by emotionally promoting Fulton's naval experiments:

> . . . I know not how far I may differ in opinion from those among you who may have turned their attention to the subject to which I now allude. . . . But I should not feel easy to lose the present occasion . . . to express my private opinion that the means of submarine attack, invented and proposed by one of our citizens, carries in itself the eventual destruction of naval tyranny. I should hope and believe, if it were taken up and adopted by our government, subjected to a rigid and regular course of experiments, open and public . . . it would save this nation from future foreign wars. . . .

It might rid the seas of all the buccaneers both great and
small that invest them; it might free mankind from the
scourge of naval wars, one of the greatest calamities they
now suffer, and to which I can see no other end. These opinions may be thought hazardous. But I beg my fellow citizens to believe that I have examined the subject, or I should
not hazard them. . . . [34]

Robert Fulton also continued to publicize his naval concepts. He wrote to his steamboat partner, Livingston:

. . . I am now writing on Torpedoes with engraved demonstrations, about the first of February [1810] I intend
going to Washington, my publication will come out so strong
and convincing that I foresee torpedoes will become our best
protection and hope, and to a certainty produce a complete
liberty of the seas—This you will say is seeing a great way
before one's nose. . . . [35]

Fulton's publication, called *Torpedo War and Submarine Explosions*, was a report on his progress to date and an outline of
his prospectus. With the help of his book and his influential
friends, Fulton's request for governmental aid for his next
"torpedo" experiment was given favorable consideration in a
congressional committee. On 17 February, as the committee
reviewed the evidence, Fulton delivered a major address to
Congress in Washington on his "torpedo" system. He displayed
some of its components, including the harpoon, the harpoon
gun, and some "torpedoes." Referring to various famous scientists and inventors of the past, he said that Roger Bacon,
Galileo, and Torricelli were brothers-in-adversity with him. He
concluded his address with an appeal for congressional support
containing not a little pathos:

. . . whatever may be your decision, whether you now
support this system and carry it into effect, or abandon it to
the chances of time; I will never forsake it but with my
breath, and I shall hope to see it become the favorite means
of protecting the commerce and liberty of my suffering country. Should I sink under the casualties of life, it will be an
orphan of the arts which I recommend to the guardianship

of my fellow citizens; let them nourish it with the care I have watched over it for nine years past.[36]

As the committee still deliberated, Secretary of the Navy Hamilton decided to put the ranking naval officer, Commodore John Rodgers, in charge of any experiment sanctioned by Congress.[37] By any standards, Rodgers was a logical choice for this assignment. His whole life had been dedicated to the sea. Serving initially in the merchant marine, he was appointed a first mate before he was eighteen years old. He was later commissioned a lieutenant in the infant U.S. Navy in 1798. Rodgers distinguished himself in fighting during the Quasi-War and the Barbary Wars, which earned him a promotion to commodore. In 1811, in the *President*, he engaged and defeated the British *Little Belt*, which action did much to alleviate United States shame over the 1807 *Chesapeake-Leopard* encounter. During the War of 1812, among other things, Rodgers defended Washington and Baltimore against the British. He was to assume several key administrative positions in the years following the war.[38]

Following Hamilton's intimation that he would be placed in charge of the torpedo experiments, Commodore Rodgers received a letter from C. W. Goldsborough, the chief clerk of the naval department, which elaborated upon Fulton's projects. Goldsborough served at the naval department from 1798 until 1843, with the exception of two years. He had developed a fairly accurate sense of congressional sentiment and believed that it would ultimately adopt Fulton's "torpedo" proposals. This did not please him, and his dislike for Fulton is apparent in the following excerpt from his letter to Rodgers:

> I am fairly certain that Mr. Fulton's system will be adopted by Congress. To me it appears visionary in the extreme—altho' not a nautical man, I can readily concur that numerous expedients might be devised to [neutralize] the effects of his Torpedoes. In my mind they are altogether unsatisfactory—tho he says that he is unprepared to encounter the ignorance of the multitude—that "little wits & babbling orators" will oppose—but in vain—for notwith-

standing such opposition he says that the name of Fulton will be remembered with reverence when all his opponents will have sunk into oblivion. . . . [39]

Federalist newspapers also opposed Robert Fulton's ideas of naval warfare. This came as no surprise to the inventor as he had always been a staunch Jeffersonian. He wrote to his most important sympathizer, now retired at Monticello, that, "All the Tories and marine or navy men are against me, they are even outrageous, for if I succeed all their hopes of Navies, armies and power with all the frippery will be blown up!" Fulton added, "When their hope of undue influence shall be forever gone, they may make good and useful citizens."[40]

On 26 February 1810, the committee made its final report to the Senate. It unanimously recommended that the government allocate an as yet undesignated sum of money for Robert Fulton to use in conducting a major experiment with his mines to "remove all doubts as to the certainty of its operation." Fulton's *Torpedo War and Submarine Explosions* was later included in the official record. In March, Fulton thanked the committee but in his correspondence with the chairman called one of his opponents "a very little man, who for want of better materials . . . cannot Instruct turns Buffoon to amuse the company, however although such triflers may be obstacles . . . it is fortunate for mankind they cannot prevent its progress."[41] It is not known to whom Fulton was referring, possibly Paul Hamilton, Goldsborough, some unknown member of Congress, or even Rodgers. The following excerpt from a letter Rodgers wrote to his wife shows that he did not regard Fulton's concept of naval warfare impartially: "It is the most . . . visionary scheme that can be conceived to have originated in the brain of a man not actually out of his senses. I am not a little astonished that Congress should have [word obscured] themselves to be so far imposed on. . . ."[42] Rodgers's opinion was directly opposed by that of Thomas Jefferson. The former president praised Fulton's plan for naval warfare in the following fashion: ". . . Your torpedoes will be to cities what vaccination has been to mankind. It extinguishes their greatest danger, but there will still be navies not for the destruction of cities, but for the plunder of commerce on the high seas. That the Tories should be against you is in character, because it will curtail the power of their idol, England."[43] A few weeks later, the former president modified his opinion further in support of Fulton's ideas. He wrote, "I sincerely wish the torpedo may go the whole length you expect of putting down navies. I wish it too much not to become an easy convert & to give it all my prayers & interest."[44]

In March 1810, Congress voted an appropriation of $5,000 for the "torpedo" experiment. Secretary Hamilton contacted Fulton about the grant and advised him that Commodore Rodgers would "conduct the defence."[45] This experiment was going to be significantly different from all of Fulton's previous tests. In the past, unmanned and unprotected ships had served as targets. This time a fully manned ship was going to be defended by an experienced and very capable seaman who had no love for Robert Fulton's type of naval warfare.

Whatever may be said of Robert Fulton, he cannot be accused of a lack of daring—or gall, depending on one's point of view. He now had the nerve to ask Hamilton to tell him specifically how the Navy planned to repel his attacks in the test. Fulton imperiously requested:

> . . . will you have the goodness to order a Circular letter to be sent to the different officers immediately, . . . [Ask] such of them as may be in this city or neighborhood to state their plan of defence to me. This becomes necessary in order that I may have a view of the difficulties which may happen to my mode of attack and have time to construct machinery to defeat them.[46]

Secretary Hamilton did not respond to this request.

Fulton also wanted an impartial but interested group of civilians to observe and report on the experiment to be conducted in New York harbor. Hamilton agreed. Accordingly, the secretary of the Navy issued invitations to New York Governor Morgan Lewis, Robert R. Livingston, Oliver Wolcott, Cadwallader Colden, and several others to attend the demonstration. Fulton could not have been unhappy with the names of the appointees, all friends of his. Hamilton also indicated that, if the New York tests were successful, a follow-up experiment would be conducted on the Potomac.[47] Fulton answered Hamilton in a few days. He did not intend to blow up a ship in New York harbor, he said, but to test tactics for approaching the ship and avoiding enemy countermeasures. He said that most of the allotted $5,000 was to be used later, presumably to buy a vessel to blow up in the projected Potomac test. Fulton closed with another political thrust, ". . . the federalists to a man Voted against the appropriation and thereby exhibited not only their Ignorance of advancing science . . . But also a total disregard for common sense . . . "[48] Fulton and Secretary Hamilton maintained close contact throughout the spring and summer on administrative matters concerning the tests.[49]

On 21 September 1810, Commodore Rodgers and his aide Captain Chauncey met with Fulton and most of the appointed civilian commissioners at the City Hotel in New York to establish the ground rules for the tests. Fulton showed the group a lock for firing and also demonstrated a model of one of his "torpedoes." Of the various tests he was going to conduct, the

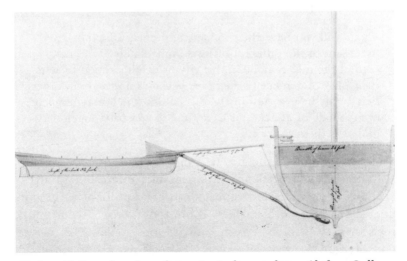

Robert Fulton drawing of spar torpedo, no date. Alofsen Collection, The New Jersey Historical Society, Alan Frazer, photographer

major one would   consist of attacking the target ship with a
blank spar torpedo, that is, an explosive charge attached to the
end of a long pole protruding from the bow of a rowboat.
Fulton said that he wanted the demonstration to be in the East
River, so that he could easily use the facilities of the navy yard
at Brooklyn. He also requested that Rodgers make the frigate
President available for the test. As the *President* was anchored
in the Hudson River, Rodgers said that he preferred to use the
Argus, already located in the East River. Fulton agreed. The
meeting adjourned, and the participants agreed to reassemble
on the twenty fourth to conduct the first test.

Unfavorable weather delayed the initial test until 25 September. Robert Fulton was undoubtedly taken aback by his first
view of the *Argus*'s defenses. Her commanding officer, Lieutenant James Lawrence—who was to cry "Don't give up the
ship!" from the bowels of the *Chesapeake* three years
later—had very effectively protected the *Argus* with a melange
of equipment including nets, grappling irons, spars and other
weights suspended from the yards, and even a crude type of
swinging scythe. Lawrence noted later that he had used no
special equipment, and that, on the second attempt, the ship

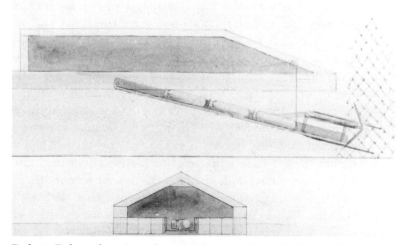

*Robert Fulton drawing of net-cutter, no date. Alofsen Collection,
The New Jersey Historical Society, Alan Frazer, photographer*

was rigged in less than fifteen minutes. The *Argus* was very effectively barricaded. Neither seaman nor spar could penetrate this wall of clanking clutter. For at least once in his life, Robert Fulton was completely nonplussed. He reported frankly to Secretary Hamilton:

> I will now do justice to the talents of Commodore Rodgers, by stating that the nets, booms, kentledge, and grappels, which he had arranged round the Argus, made, at first sight, a formidable appearance against *one torpedo boat and eight bad oarsmen*. I was taken unawares: I had explained to the officers of the navy my means of attack; they did not inform me of their measures of defence. . . .[50]

Fulton would later propose schemes to circumvent Rodgers's and Lawrence's defenses. He envisioned a combination of knives, fired from a boat gun, to cut a hole in the defensive net. The "torpedoes" would then be released through that hole, in Fulton's words, "in the same manner as potatoes are commonly emptied from the body of a cart."[51] He never carried out this plan. The simple truth was that Robert Fulton had failed in the most important single test in the series that he conducted over several days.

Several other of his tests, although less significant than this first one, failed as well. An initial attempt to cut an anchor cable did not succeed, and the harpoon gun proved to be effective at no more than fifteen feet. This meant that in combat the boat crew would be within extremely close range of enemy small arms fire. On 28 September, as if to emphasize the vulnerability of the "torpedo" boat crew, Captain Chauncey anchored a small craft ninety feet from the pier. He ordered three pieces of loose board to be placed upright in the boat to resemble three men and "discharged a grape" at this target. Upon examination, it was found that eighteen shot penetrated the first board, nine the second, five the third, and seventy-three pieces hit the boat. Chauncey had made his point, although Fulton argued that, as the harpoon gun had proved effective at fifteen feet, with modifications its distance from the target could be increased.

Despite these setbacks, Fulton did conduct successfully some important experiments in 1810. On 1 November, a device for cutting anchor lines successfully severed a fourteen-inch anchor cable several inches below the surface. As the cutting mechanism had been fired by discharging powder under water, this test proved that a shell could pass through water. A later test, however, indicated there were still many details to be worked out in this procedure.

Unfortunately, the majority of Fulton's peers did not recognize the significance of this achievement. Nor did most realize the potential value of what Fulton called the "anchored torpedo," really the prototype of the modern moored mine. Fulton attached one of these mines to a weighted anchor and

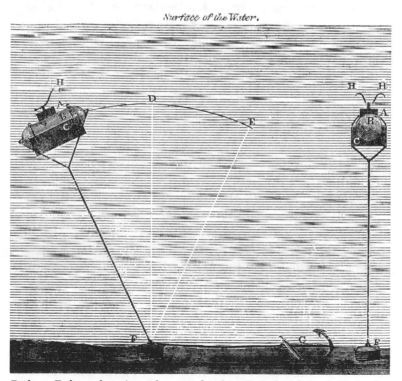

Robert Fulton drawing of moored mine. Reprinted from Torpedo War and Submarine Explosions, *Plate II*

planted it in the East River off the navy yard, where it remained for several days. Then, when the commissioners examined it, they found it in the desired vertical position unaf-
fected by tidal changes. Commodore Rodgers attempted to
minimize this success by pointing out that the mine's explosive
capabilities had not been tested. Fulton tartly replied, "Let me
put one under water, and they who do not believe in its effect,
may put their confidence to the proof by sailing over it." No
one did. Fulton was especially pleased with the economy of his
"anchored torpedo." As compared to using a warship for defense, which cost then approximately $200,000 to $300,000 to
construct, each mine cost only between eight hundred and one
thousand dollars. In February 1811 he urged Secretary of the
Navy Hamilton to place them in defensive positions in the major eastern bays and harbors. The moored mine was the most
economical and practical of all of Robert Fulton's naval inventions. If governmental leaders had recognized the value of Fulton's discovery and used it accordingly, it is conceivable that in
the forthcoming War of 1812, the nation's capital might not
have been captured and burned, Baltimore might not have
been attacked, and indeed, the national anthem might not
have been written!

Despite the successful test of the "anchored torpedo," the
commissioners' report on the 1810 New York experiment concluded that "Mr. Fulton has not, in the opinion of a majority of
the committee, proved that the government ought to rely upon
his system as a means of national defence."[52] Apparently the
failure of the *Argus* test had been the overriding factor in their
decision. At a time when his steamboats were becoming increasingly popular with the public, Fulton's naval inventions
fell into temporary disfavor.

Bitterly disappointed, Fulton became involved for a time
with his other projects. Having outlined earlier an extensive
plan for a major canal traversing Pennsylvania, he now wrote
his friends urging a system of canals in the United States.
Fulton saw canals as a means of "cementing the union," as he
put it. Undoubtedly with the recent Aaron Burr conspiracy in
mind he wrote:

Intrigues have been practiced to sever the western from
the eastern states. . . . [but] when the United States shall be
bound together by canals, by a sense of mutual interests aris-
ing from mutual intercourse and mingled commerce, it will
be no more possible to split them into independent and separate governments . . . than it is now possible for the government of England to divide and form again into seven
kingdoms.[53]

In New York Fulton had become good friends with De Witt
Clinton, then mayor of the city, and in May 1811 Fulton was
designated a member of a special commission that was to consider the feasibility of a canal in the upper regions of the state.
Other members included Clinton, Robert Livingston, and the
American diplomat and statesman Gouverneur Morris. Fulton
primarily worked at promoting the New York state canal, ar-
guing that it would be more profitable than alternate methods
of transportation. Indeed, it has even been argued that Fulton
was initially more zealous in this effort than De Witt Clinton.[54]

Most of his time during this period was spent developing his
steamboat operations. Angry Hudson River steamboat captains, probably fearing potential competition and disliking this
new steam-driven ship, had created an earlier problem when
they tried to ram Fulton's steamboat and disable her paddlewheels. The steamboat prevailed, however, and Fulton soon
added others to accompany the *North River Steam Boat* (or
Steam Boat). Representative of his newer boats was the
Paragon, by 1812 the queen of the river. One of Fulton's cosmopolitan artist friends, a Russian named Paul Svinin, described her thusly:

. . . The interior is divided into two sections: one for
women, the other for men. The first consists of two large
cabins, one for sleeping, with sixteen berths and eight sofas,
the other a dining-saloon, furnished with twenty berths and
ten sofas. In addition there is in this section a water-closet
and a pantry. . . . In the fore-part of the boat there is a fine
cabin for the captain, offices for the engineer, and servants'
quarters. The kitchen is very remarkable both for its cleanliness and its location: all the cooking and frying is done with

*Statue of Robert Fulton and his steamboat in the Hall of Statues,
U.S. Capitol. Architect of the Capitol*

the aid of steam, and every day food for 150 persons is prepared with great ease. The order and cleanliness are aston-
ishing! Gleaming silver and bronze, shining mirrors and ma-
hogany are everywhere, and the most refined taste can find
here everything to his liking; the best wines, all manner of
dainties, and even ice-cream in the hot season.[55]

Fulton was increasingly satisfied with each successive steamboat. He wrote exultantly to a business acquaintance Thomas
Law, on 16 April, "My Paragon Beats everything on this globe,
for mad as you and I are we cannot tell what is in the moon."[56]

Late in 1811, Fulton sent his steamboat the *New Orleans*
down the Ohio River from Pittsburgh for the port for which
she was named. Her captain was Nicholas J. Roosevelt. Several
weeks later, following an earthquake, a birth (Roosevelt's wife
was pregnant but insisted on accompanying her husband), and
several other emergencies, Fulton's steamboat docked at New
Orleans. This was the first steamboat on the western waters of
the Ohio and Mississippi Rivers. Henry Clay recalled, "With
regard to the Mississippi, a new epoch has been produced in its
navigation by the genius of Fulton."[57]

Robert Fulton's activities were endless. New York commu-
ters (they existed even in the early 1800s) persuaded him to
build steam ferry boats for both the Hudson and East Rivers.
His first steam ferry on the East River between Manhattan and
Brooklyn was called *Nassau*. She was a catamaran, with a deck
wide enough to carry saddle horses and wagons, as well as foot
passengers. The paddlewheel was placed between the two
hulls. On a bigger scale, this would also be the design for his
steam warship (see next chapter). After Fulton died, both the
Manhattan and Brooklyn streets leading to his ferry slips would
be renamed "Fulton Street" in his honor. Fulton also continued
painting, designed bridges, built an extensive machine and
steam engine shop in Jersey City, and even had time to expose
some frauds. Probably the most striking of these involved a
man named Redheffer, who demonstrated what he called a
"perpetual motion" device in New York. Fulton observed the
machine, but suspected that there was something wrong. De-

spite the angry remonstrations of Redheffer, Fulton knocked aside some coverings and exposed a hidden partner of Redheffer's turning a crank to move the supposedly perpetually moving machine. Redheffer fled in disgrace, and Fulton moved up another notch in the public's estimation. Fulton never lost interest, however, in his primary concern in life, the development of his naval inventions and concepts of naval warfare.

As American diplomatic relations with both France and England worsened, Robert Fulton maintained his contacts with former associates in both countries. He sent copies of his book, *Torpedo War and Submarine Explosions*, to friends in both lands, but his remarks accompanying these gifts indicate a solid preference for France. He told his former French colleagues, Volney, Monge, and Laplace, that he wished to see "the Genius of the Emperor relieved from the fatigues of war."[58] On the other hand, he angrily admonished Lord Stanhope that "The depridations [*sic*] of your fleets in our commerce and the Injustice of your government towards these States Cries aloud for such coercion as shall produce a reform."[59] This passage implies that Fulton intended his book to be this very "coercion." The fact that a portion of the book described tactics for mounting a "torpedo" attack from France against England cannot have endeared him to his English readers. In the book, he envisioned 2,000 French "torpedo" boats inhibiting English naval power "from Boulogne . . . to the mouth of the Thames."[60]

In May 1811, Commodore Rodgers in the *President* closed with and damaged the British sloop *Little Belt*. Americans applauded this endeavor, viewing it as revenge for the *Chesapeake* affair four years earlier; relations between the two English-speaking countries were disintegrating dangerously. Perhaps inspired by Rodgers's action, Fulton now sent an agent to France to attempt again to interest Napoleon in using his naval weapons against the British. While offering weapons to an unfriendly country was probably not in the best interest of the United States, nothing came of it. Fulton certainly had no doubts which side he was on, and when war was finally declared with Britain in June 1812, he was very desirous of playing a major role in it.

It soon became apparent that Paul Hamilton was not capable of serving as head of the wartime Navy Department. Early in 1813, he was replaced by William Jones, a mariner and Philadelphia merchant. The opposite of his predecessor, Jones had extensive nautical experience and was a firm and decisive administrator who stressed coordination within the navy. He was unique in his ability to work well with both the traditionally conservative senior naval officers and imaginative innovators like Fulton. During his two-year period as secretary, Jones removed Goldsborough and reorganized the department to his own liking. William Jones is generally recognized as one of the best secretaries of the navy in American history.[61] Fulton himself wrote, "The high character which I have ever heard of Mr. Jones, his penetration and friendship for the useful arts, gave me every reason to calculate on his warm support. . . ."[62]

With the new and supportive naval chief, Fulton enthusiastically set to work to improve his naval weapons and employ them in the war effort. Jefferson sent Fulton encouragement, telling him, "I rejoice at the success of your steamboat. . . . I hope your torpedoes will equally triumph over doubting friends and presumptuous enemies."[63] Fulton worked on a variety of possible tactics for "torpedo" boats, stressing night attack, muffling the oars, and proper clothing to avoid being observed by the enemy. He wanted the crews to dress in: ". . . white flannel over waistcoats and white flannel caps . . . and expose nothing but their faces for almost pure white is the colour which on the water is most difficult to be seen in the night. if the night be very dark no colour can be seen if gray or usually dark white receives a gray tint the colour of the water and sky."[64] With his artistic background, it appears that Fulton appreciated some of the subtleties of the art of camouflage. Fulton soon contacted Secretary Jones, urging the use of his weapons for coastal and harbor defense. He also requested a patent for his naval inventions from Secretary of State James

Monroe.[65] It is not certain, however, if he ever received this.

Fulton's naval activities increased as the war progressed. He furnished his weapons to American naval officers in the Great Lakes theatre, although these were apparently never used there, one reason being that they were no longer needed after American Commander Oliver Hazard Perry's decisive victory in the Battle of Lake Erie in September 1813. Fulton also experimented with the electrical firing of underwater explosives, but little is known of his actual achievements in this area.[66]

War in the United States did not affect Fulton domestically. On one occasion he wrote to his steamboat partner that "Mrs. Livingston is with us . . . and we are happy as doves in a basket."[67] However, a double tragedy was soon to occur for the American inventor. Joel Barlow had undertaken a diplomatic mission abroad that resulted in his accompanying Napoleon on his drive towards Russia. Barlow became ill in Poland and died in 1812. Ruth Barlow was inconsolable and finally moved in with the Fultons for an extended stay. Jefferson wrote to Fulton, "I sincerely condole with you on the death of our much lamented friend Barlow. . . . I consider the loss as irreparable to our country when I look for the man capable of writing it's [sic] history."[68] On 26 February 1813, Robert R. Livingston died. Thus, within two months, Fulton had lost both his philosophical mentor and his steamboat partner.

American enthusiasm and support for "torpedo" warfare grew during 1813. One press account called for the establishment of a "Torpedo Corps," and stated:

> The much ridiculed torpedo is obtaining a high reputation. It seems reduced to a certainty that they may be used with wonderful effect. Those who laughed at them, *elegantly* and constantly vociferating "Quiz Torpedo Fudge!" now, "sweet gentle souls," preach to us about the *morality* of using them. . . . The enemy fights in the *air* with his rockets—he fights *under the earth* with his mines, and yet *he* is hugely "religious." May it not then become "a moral and religious people," like *we* are, to fight *under the water,* with torpedoes and diving boats.[69]

Congress had already responded on 3 March 1813 with the

passage of the so-called "Torpedo Act," which ruled that any person who destroyed a British ship be paid one half the value of that ship. More significantly, Congress authorized Americans "to use torpedoes, submarines instruments, or any other destructive machine whatever."[70] Undoubtedly in response to the "Torpedo Act" of 1813, American "torpedo" activity in combat increased in that year. At least three American "torpedo" boats operated in eastern waters. None of these boats accomplished any real damage to the enemy in combat, but they probably did have a detrimental psychological effect on the British. Although the British blamed most of this activity on Robert Fulton, it is unlikely that any of the boats were his. Fulton's torpedoes were used, however, to harass the British. At this time, ships of the Royal Navy were patrolling the Chesapeake Bay at will, severely impeding American commerce. An article in the Annapolis-published *Maryland Gazette* on 4 March 1813 called attention to Fulton's naval weapons and hoped they would be used against the British ships in the Chesapeake region.[71] A Chesapeake mariner named Elijah Mix responded to the article and volunteered his services to the Navy Department. Benjamin Latrobe, the architect later engaged to rebuild the Capitol after its destruction by the British in 1814, had discovered some of Fulton's old European "torpedoes" lying loose in a Washington building and told Fulton and Secretary Jones of his find. Jones, with Fulton's concurrence, put the mines at Elijah Mix's disposal.[72]

Mix's primary target for Fulton's mines was the seventy-four-gun HMS *Plantaganet* guarding the mouth of the Chesapeake Bay near Cape Henry. On one occasion Mix maneuvered his rowboat to within twelve yards of the *Plantagenet*, but was spotted before he could set the mine and hastily withdrew under fire. On another occasion, the night of 24 July, Mix set the mechanism and threw the mine overboard some distance from the *Plantaganet*. The tide carried it towards its target, but the mine exploded before it reached its destination. It sent a giant column of water up into the air which splashed on the deck of the British ship, frightening the crew, but damage was minimal. The major effect of all of Mix's raids was that the British were forced to maintain a higher state of readiness against attack in the Chesapeake.

The primary British target in the New York area was the HMS *Ramilies*, under the command of Captain Thomas Hardy. Hardy is best remembered as the captain of the HMS *Victory*, Lord Nelson's flagship at Trafalgar, and as Nelson's friend, who comforted him after he had been mortally wounded. The *Ramilies* operated in Long Island Sound, generally close to New London, Connecticut. Reports of American "torpedo" boats in the vicinity are sketchy and difficult to verify. The first indication of an American attack was a July 1813 press announcement:

> . . . We understand a gentleman at Norwich has invented a diving boat, which by means of paddles he can propel underwater at the rate of three miles an hour and asend [*sic*] and descend at pleasure. He has made a number of experiments, and been three times under the bottom of the Ramilies, off New London. . . . In the third attempt he came up directly under the Ramilies, and fastened himself and his boat to her keel, where he remained half an hour, and succeeded in perforating a hole through her copper, and while engaged in screwing a torpedo to her bottom, the screw broke, and defeated his object for that time. So great is the alarm and fear on board the "Ramilies" that com. Hardy has withdrawn his force from before New London, and keeps his ship underway all the time. . . .[73]

It is not known for sure if the "gentleman at Norwich" did indeed attack the *Ramilies*, but Captain Hardy certainly was upset over "torpedoes" in general. He issued the following orders to a subordinate:

> Having received positive information that a whaleboat, the property of Thomas Welling and others, prepared with a torpedo, for the avowed purpose of sinking this ship, a mode of warfare practised [*sic*] by individuals from mercenary motives and more novel than honorable, is kept in your neighborhood and as . . . there is no doubt these persons will

soon be in my power, I beg you to warn the inhabitants of the towns along the coast of Long-Island, that whenever I hear of this boat or any other of her description has been allowed to remain after this day, I will order every house near the shore to be destroyed.[74]

The most famous "torpedo" boat on Long Island Sound was the so-called "Turtle Boat," which had a short but dramatic career. This strange craft seems to have been a combination of submarine and surface vessel. The lower part resembled the part of a boat that travels just below the surface, and the upper part was covered with iron plating. As that was all that was visible, it must have indeed resembled a turtle shell. The craft reportedly could hold a crew of twelve. The "Turtle Boat" began operations on the Sound in 1814, but before she did any damage, she ran aground on the northeastern shore of Long Island near Southold. Although the British attempted to destroy the hulk on the beach, native Long Islanders were able to engage the enemy long enough to destroy the craft themselves in order to prevent the British from seeing her mechanisms. Because a British officer called it "the wonderful turtle boat, which has been so long constructing at New York by the celebrated Mr. Fulton," some writers have assumed that this semi-submersible was his.[75] Two facts disprove this. One is that Fulton was indeed constructing a vessel in New York, but it was a very large steam frigate (See the following chapter). This giant craft also had a thick protective covering, somewhat resembling the famous "turtle boat" type of large warship used by the Koreans against the invading Japanese in the late sixteenth century.[76] These Korean ships had decks covered with iron plates to deflect shot, spikes to inhibit boarders, and are generally regarded as the first armored warships. The second argument against the Turtle being Fulton's boat is that the press account of the 1814 "Turtle Boat's" destruction on Long Island closed with the statement, "The boat we understand is the invention of an ingenious gentleman by the name of Berrian."[77] Nevertheless, the British continued to blame Fulton and once allegedly even mounted an operation to attempt to capture him. Captain Hardy also shelled the Connecticut town of Stonington because he believed it was a storage area for Fulton's weapons.

One significant thing Robert Fulton did accomplish during this period was to become friends with Captain Stephen Decatur, a heroic figure famed for his daring exploits in the Tripoli War. Decatur's ship, the *United States*, was so big that she was nicknamed "The Wagon," presumably the origin of the modern slang term for a major capital ship, "battlewagon." Robert Fulton's work and friendship with Stephen Decatur belies the traditional belief that Fulton could not get along with senior naval officers. In 1813 Fulton had been experimenting with what he called a "submarine gun" or "Columbiad." Fulton described this new invention very simply: "Instead of placing the cannon in a vessel as usual above the surface of the water, I arrange my cannon so low that they will be below the surface. The bullets will pass through the water instead of through air,

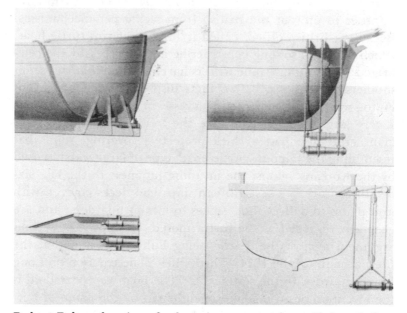

Robert Fulton drawing of submarine gun, no date. Alofsen Collection, The New Jersey Historical Society, Alan Frazer, photographer

and through the side of the enemy's vessel below the surface, which letting in water will sink the vessel."[78] It is ironic that Fulton never used the term "torpedo" to describe this weapon, because the submarine gun appears to be more similar to the modern torpedo than do Fulton's "torpedoes." Unexpectedly, Fulton received some aid from his new friend. On 6 May 1813, Captain Decatur wrote an extended testimonial in full support not only of Fulton's submarine gun but also of his old cable-cutter of the 1810 New York experiment, which Decatur believed was a practical invention too. The captain concluded with a statement that would have terrified Commodore Rodgers: ". . . I perfectly agree with Mr. Fulton, that Should his experiments prove that the [submarine gun] can be fired as he contemplates, and as I have much reason to believe, this new mode of Maritime warfare must anihilate [sic] the present System, by rendering Small vessels equal to large ones, for both must Sink if attacked in a like manner."[79] This important testimonial was only the beginning of a pleasant and fruitful association between Decatur and the inventor. Two days later, on 8 May, Fulton and Decatur signed an agreement to split both the expenses and the profits resulting from the development of the submarine gun. Fulton would do the work, and Decatur would "use all the means in his power . . . to carry the said invention into practical use."[80] Fulton sent Decatur's testimonial to Thomas Jefferson on 8 July. The former president enthusiastically responded that he had forwarded Decatur's comments to President Madison along with a strong recommendation that the government support the submarine gun. Jefferson also reminded Fulton that he had never forgotten his first major naval invention in France. Jefferson wrote, "I confess I have more hopes of the mode of destruction by the submarine boat, than any other."[81] On 5 August 1813, Fulton corresponded with Decatur on a variety of subjects. His vague queries on the New London "torpedo" attacks are further evidence that Fulton was not directly involved in these operations. On 4 September Fulton described a radical new method of "torpedo" attack to Decatur. Fulton drew a diagram of a friendly vessel supporting two very long spar torpedoes several feet below its keel, which were to be rammed under the hull of the enemy vessel.[82] Fulton and Decatur were also working very closely on a great steam frigate, but that will be covered in the next chapter.

Even Commodore Rodgers was now getting along better with Fulton. Visiting the naval officer at his Baltimore home on 8 and 9 September 1814, Fulton exhibited to him "models of the mode of suspending torpedoes" and left him two lock and clock mechanisms.[83] The inventor then returned to New York, just missing the historic British bombardment of Fort McHenry. On the very morning that Francis Scott Key wrote his immortal words, Fulton wrote to his old nemesis Rodgers:

> The news here is that the enemy are in great force at the entrance of the [word obscured] if so let down the . . . torpedoes among them in the night. . . . Now perhaps is a favorable time for some of your young officers and a few good crews in boats to distinguish themselves and render an important service to their country. . . . Apply the whole force of your genius as much to blow up the British as you did to oppose me and you will succeed. if you have time drop me a line how things are and whether I can be of any service to you. . . .[84]

Old animosities were forgotten when the nation was in peril.

Robert Fulton engaged in still other naval activities in 1814. He corresponded with Captain Chauncey concerning naval tactics on the Great Lakes. Fulton also released his steamboats for use as transports of both troops and supplies during the war. But his most significant accomplishment in 1814 was the construction of his steam frigate *Demologos*, or, as it was later designated by the Navy, *Fulton the First*.

5

"Fulton the First"

In the final years of his life, Robert Fulton would design and supervise the construction of the first steam warship in history. Just as he would be the first man to develop steam warship technology, he would also be the first inventor to request a cabinet level position in the U.S. government for himself.

As the British increased their naval operations in eastern waters in 1813, Americans defending the harbors became increasingly concerned and searched for new ways to counter the enemy's attacks. Fulton's "torpedoes" were being used in both offensive and defensive operations but without much success. Then, during the early summer of 1813, Fulton developed the concept of a large and heavily armed steam warship.

Although the exact origin of Fulton's idea for this vessel is unknown, it appears to have been, in part, an outgrowth of his work with Stephen Decatur on the submarine gun. When Fulton sent Decatur's testimonial on the submarine gun to Thomas Jefferson in July 1813, he wrote to the ex-president that approval "from so experienced an officer must have weight with those who are not familiar with nautical affairs." He also said, "The object now is to give a fair experiment to this discovery By building a Vessel and fitting her in the best manner to secure success." Fulton then asked Jefferson to lobby for a Congressional appropriation of $100,000 for this vessel.[1] This large sum greatly exceeded Fulton's previous requests for his other naval projects and suggests that the vessel in question was indeed the prototype of the large steam warship.

Stephen Decatur played a very important role in the initial development of Fulton's steam warship. The two men wrote to one another several times during the summer of 1813, the usual pattern being that Fulton would propose an idea and Decatur would react to it. Decatur, however, sometimes initiated ideas of his own, usually related to possible operational or combat situations. In fact, it was Decatur's recognition of a possible problem that resulted in Fulton's proposal for a vessel motivated by steam rather than sail. Decatur was concerned that the masts of the American sailing vessel, which would have to go very close to the British ship for a successful submarine gun assault, would become entangled in the enemy's yards. Fulton proposed a vessel that normally would operate under sail but which could have its masts lowered and be converted to steam when nearing the enemy for the final attack with the submarine gun. The inventor put it this way, "Steam can bring the Vessel close within 12 or 6 feet and can carry her off out of danger after her fire is given."[2] Although Decatur believed that Fulton's idea would solve the problem of mast entanglement, he was also concerned that the closeness of the two ships might allow the enemy to board the steam warship. As a solution, he proposed designing a "considerable slope" to the deck and covering it with sharp iron spikes set three inches apart. To the obvious question of how the American crew was going to walk on their own deck, Decatur responded simply, "This deck we could keep covered with boards until going alongside of the enemy."[3] Fulton also considered using a pump that could shoot big jets of pressurized water at an enemy ship several hundred feet away, although apparently this was never tested. It is unlikely that this water-jet pump or Decatur's spiked deck were included in the ship when it was finally built. It is possible, however, that the iron stanchions installed on the ship's deck may have given onlookers the impression of spiked decks for defense.[4] Later reports of this spiked deck may have accounted for the British allusion to Fulton's "turtle boat" described in Chapter Four.

Almost imperceptibly, Fulton's interest had shifted from the submarine gun to the steam warship. By November 1813, he had sketched out the transverse, top, and side views of the steam warship. Depicting a heavily armed ship, he placed eight cannon on either side of the vessel, as well as two each fore and aft. The paddlewheel was located in the center of the ship, with the boiler placed on its port side and the engine placed on its starboard side. Both the boiler and engine were situated below the waterline, which represented a radical departure from Fulton's earlier steamboat models whose engines had been on deck.[5] The finished vessel would incorporate all of the basic features of these initial drawings.

The confusing history of the changing names of Robert Fulton's steam warship has been traced by David B. Tyler. Although historians have generally referred to this vessel as *Demologos*, or "Voice of the People," Tyler notes that Fulton only used that name once, in the aforementioned drawings of November 1813. During the following month, while legal papers were being drawn up, the vessel was referred to as *Pyremon*, "vomiting fire." The ship was thereafter usually assigned names of a more general nature, such as *Steam Battery*, *Floating Battery*, *Steam Frigate* or *Fulton Steam Frigate*. When the vessel was launched in October 1814, the Navy named her *Fulton the First*. While Tyler feels that *Fulton Steam Frigate* was the official designation later, *Fulton the First* was apparently deemed a more appropriate name at the time of launching because it indicated that Robert Fulton had designed the first steam warship in history.[6]

By the fall of 1813, Fulton and Decatur had gradually transformed their original concept of the steam vessel from that of an offensive warship to that of a more sedentary floating blockship designed for harbor defense. Fulton was particularly worried about the defense of New York Bay. Undoubtedly his motives were not entirely unselfish, as most of his steamboats, his Jersey City engine shop, and several other small and largely personal enterprises were located in the immediate vicinity. Moreover, there are two water approaches to New York. The British had their choice of sailing up into New York Bay through the narrows separating Brooklyn from Staten Island, or they could sail westward on Long Island Sound and enter the East River from the north. Fulton believed that his steam warship would be particularly well suited to respond to a threat from either direction, as the ship could be easily moved from one location to another.

In December 1813, Fulton invited several prominent gentlemen to help him organize the wartime protection of New York's waterways. These men, who included former Secretary of War Henry Dearborn, Oliver Wolcott, Samuel L. Mitchill, Adam Brown, Thomas Morris, Cadwallader Colden, Henry Rutgers, Morgan Lewis, and Stephen Decatur, met at Fulton's New York home on Christmas Eve. Fulton briefly described to the gathering his contemplated steam warship, explaining that it was to be exactly as depicted in his November drawings except for the addition of four more guns. The inventor then proposed that the group organize as a company to develop the vessel. All agreed and the Coast and Harbor Defence Company was thus founded. With Dearborn selected as president and Fulton named engineer, the immediate goal of the new company was to obtain financial backing to pay for construction of the vessel.[7]

Stephen Decatur returned to his base at New London where he again pondered the exigencies of a combat situation. The battle-experienced officer now devised a new technique (although it is doubtful if it was ever used) to frustrate enemy sailors who might attempt to board the American vessel:

> A single mode of defending your vessel from boarding from the enemy's boats has suggested itself to me, to-wit: an iron rail of two inches in diameter to run round the vessel close down to the water's edge, supported from the vessel's sides by iron-braces, and thrown off say eight or ten feet from the vessel's sides. No boat could then get alongside.[8]

More significantly, Decatur persuaded most of his fellow senior naval officers in the New London area to support Fulton's new concept. On 3 January 1814, Decatur, along with Captain Jacob Jones and Commander James Biddle, wrote a testimonial on behalf of Fulton's steam warship. They stated that the design indicated that "her sides are so thick as to be impenetrable to every kind of shot," and that the ship would "be rendered more formidable to an enemy than any kind of engine hitherto invented." In general extolling the virtues of Fulton's vessel, the three naval officers recommended that the government "carry this plan into immediate execution." Six

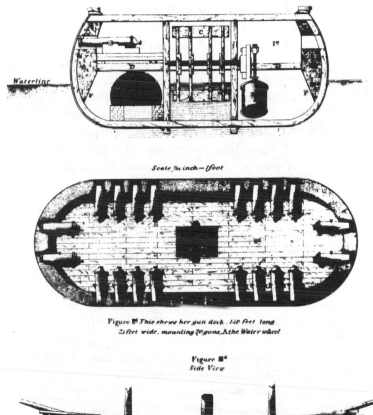

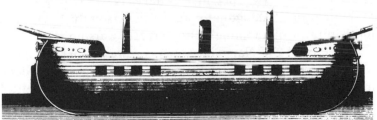

Three views of Fulton's steam warship, 1813. U.S. Naval Institute

days later Captain Oliver Hazard Perry and three additional senior naval officers added their names to this enthusiastic endorsement.[9] The wholehearted support of so many distinguished naval personages indicated that opposition to Fulton's naval projects such as that led by Rodgers and Goldsborough no longer existed. Correspondence suggests that Decatur should get much of the credit for this new era of goodwill towards Fulton.

Robert Fulton lost no time in forwarding the testimonial to Secretary of the Navy William Jones, along with a committee report from the New York Coast and Harbor Defence Company calling for financial support from the government. The committee requested an appropriation "not exceeding $320,000 or about the sum requisite for a Frigate of the first class."[10] Even before submitting this official request, Fulton began lobbying with selected governmental leaders. He wrote to Secretary of State James Monroe: "To prove those works without loss of time is of infinite importance. The President, you and Mr. Dallas can in an hour order all the money arrangements with Treasury Notes."[11] On 15 January, Fulton sent a copy of the naval officers' testimonial to Speaker of the House Henry Clay and sought his support for financial aid from Congress.[12] Clay replied that he had forwarded Fulton's correspondence to William Lowndes, the House Naval Committee chairman, and that, "The subject has attracted much attention. I have not seen one (and I have conversed with many) who is not fully persuaded of its immense importance. And I have not a doubt of Congress making provision for testing. . . . "[13] Clay concluded by saying that he planned to visit Fulton in New York in February. Next, Oliver Hazard Perry went to Washington to present in person the naval argument in favor of adopting Fulton's steam warship.[14]

Secretary of the Navy Jones was convinced that the steam warship project was practicable. He forwarded pertinent documents in his possession to Lowndes and the House committee, noting that "the certificate of Captains Decatur, Evans, Jones, Perry, Biddle and Warrington . . . leaves little room for doubt. . . . I have, therefore, no hesitation in recommending the adoption of Mr. Fulton's plan."[15]

Lowndes's counterpart in the Senate asked Secretary Jones to draft an appropriations bill. Jones responded with a request for $250,000 to build the steam warship. The Senate committee then increased this sum to $500,000 and submitted it to the Senate for a vote where it passed without opposition. After a brief discussion, the House also approved this sum, and the act authorizing one half a million dollars for the construction of Fulton's vessel became law on 9 March 1814. Robert Fulton had reached the high point of his seventeen years of naval negotiations with three major nations.

Despite this triumph, Fulton was impatient and requested immediate authorization to begin construction in New York. Two weeks after the appropriations act was passed, Fulton complained directly to President Madison about the delay:

> . . . I have been extremely anxious to commence work . . .
> but I have not yet heard from the Secretary of the Navy giv-
> ing me orders to proceed or where to find funds Should
> there not be money in the treasury for the purpose I can
> make the loan in New York on the guarantee of the govern-
> ment and any interest over 7 percent . . . presuming that
> one word from you will give Vigor to the operations, please
> to consider this letter private. . . . [16]

Fulton's last sentence above is probably explained by the fact that he respected naval secretary Jones and did not want to anger him by passing over his authority. Jones, an experienced seaman, was very much interested in this project, particularly in the technical aspects of the ship. He wrote to Fulton making several suggestions, although he was aware of Fulton's sensitivity to criticism. On one occasion, after proposing several modifications, Jones stated to Fulton, "You will pardon these suggestions; they are merely offered to be obviated by the fertility of your genius."[17] Jones's letter of 6 May 1814 to Fulton indicates that he had bookkeeping problems which were delaying transmittal of the funds, but on 23 May he gave his permission to begin construction of the steam warship.

Fulton's warship was to be constructed in two phases. First, Adam and Noah Brown would build the hull at their shipyard on the East River. The vessel was then to be towed to Fulton's engine shop on the Hudson River at Jersey City for machinery installation and completion.

Fulton's selection of Adam and Noah Brown as his builders was fortunate. The Brown brothers—no relation to *North River Steam Boat*-builder Charles Brownne—were probably the most active and knowledgeable American shipbuilders during the War of 1812. They had responded to the crisis in an exemplary fashion with a crash shipbuilding program on the Great Lakes that contributed substantially to Oliver Hazard Perry's victory there. They also constructed several large warships at their New York yard. After receiving the contract for Fulton's project, the Browns estimated the cost of the basic carpenters' work, plus metal work on the frame, to be $69,800.[18] Once the initial government funds were released, and the contracts completed, the Browns went to work.

Fulton's steamship was to be a twin-hulled vessel, or catamaran, and its two keels were laid on 20 June 1814. The inventor had earlier designed a twin-hulled steam ferry boat which operated on the Hudson between New Jersey and Manhattan in 1812.[19] He probably used this design again on his steam warship not only because it increased the ship's maneuverability but also, more importantly, because it provided protection for the paddlewheel and machinery. With this type of construction, the paddlewheel was placed in the center of the ship between the two hulls with only a small portion visible above the deck, and this was covered by a stepped wooden protective sheathing. Two boilers were located deep within one hull, and the steam engine within the other. The outer sides of the ship were paneled with solid oak roughly five feet thick. The boilers, the steam engine, and the paddlewheel were thus located below the waterline and within the massive sides of the vessel. Rarely had the workings of any vessel been so well protected up to this time.

In March 1814, Fulton indicated the ship's specifications, which included 120-foot keels, a deck 138 feet long, and a

55-foot beam. Each hull of the catamaran was to have a 20-foot beam, which would allow for a 15-foot separation between the two hulls. Fulton planned for a crew of 500, although when the ship was actually constructed there was not enough living space for this many men. With a 130-horsepower engine, the ship was to have a maximum speed of 4 to 5 knots.

Knowledge of the ship's actual appearance was sketchy up until 1960 when three plans of the vessel were discovered in the Danish Royal Archives. These plans enabled the Smithsonian Institution staff to reconstruct a model of the ship, which is presently on display in the Museum of History and Technology. Howard I. Chapelle of the Smithsonian Institution published these findings in 1964, going into more minute technical detail than would be possible in this more general work.[20]

The Browns worked at breakneck speed throughout the summer of 1814. However, funds from Washington were not coming in fast enough. To compound the problem, the British

Model of Fulton's steam warship on display at the Museum of History and Technology, Smithsonian Institution. Smithsonian Institution

had begun their offensive in the Chesapeake Bay region, and, late in August, following the battle of Bladensburg, they entered and burned the nation's capital. Small wonder that Fulton's request for funds had not been satisfied! Henry Rutgers, who had replaced Dearborn as president of the Coast and Harbor Defence Company, wrote to Secretary of the Navy Jones: "Sensibly impressed with the disaster at Washington, and the temporary embarrassment it must occasion to Government, we cannot expect for your usual attention to our pressing necessities. We have therefore deemed it expedient to send Mr. Fulton to confer with you. . . . "[21]

Fulton left New York on 1 September and arrived in Washington on the third. The inventor was deeply impressed with the charred sights of the nation's capital. He wrote to President Madison:

> . . . Believing that you feel as I do towards the new work, I may remark that one steam Ship in the Potomac might probably have saved Washington, by preventing the army calculating on the co-operation of the fleet. It could at least have saved Alexandria, and the honor of the Nation so far as that enterprise of the enemy has tarnished it.[22]

Fulton saw Secretary Jones on the afternoon of the third, and was assured that $40,000 was on the way. Departing Washington the next day, Fulton went down the Potomac about twenty miles to visit Captain David Porter. In early 1813, while commanding the *Essex*, Porter had crippled the British whaling fleet in the Pacific. Fulton observed that Porter had a "battery" (probably a small gun) facing the river, and the captain told him that he occasionally fired this at British vessels to annoy them.[23] Fulton had not visited Porter just by chance. On 8 September, Secretary Jones officially ordered Porter to "proceed to New York and take command of the steam vessel of war. . . . "[24] Fulton was undoubtedly aware of the secretary's decision when he visited Porter four days earlier.

Proceeding to New York, Captain Porter probably lodged temporarily with his friend, author Washington Irving. He took command of the ship in the final stages of hull construction at the Browns' shipyard. On 29 October 1814, the new captain reported to Secretary Jones:

> I have the honor to inform you that the United States' Fulton the First, was this morning safely launched. . . . She promises fair to meet our sanguine expectations, and I do not despair of being able to navigate in her from one extreme of our coast to the other. Her buoyancy astonishes every one . . . her draft will only be ten feet with all her guns, machinery, stores and crew on board.[25]

The steam warship was later to be rigged with sails, largely due to a request from Porter. The Browns had built the *Fulton the First* in less than five months, a Herculean effort. The British attack and burning of Washington undoubtedly caused many New Yorkers to fear that they might be next, which in turn probably accelerated the ship's construction. On the other hand, the vessel was such a novelty that curious onlookers sometimes got in the workmens' way, and the shipyard's security force had to be increased. A large crowd assembled and watched as the vessel was transferred from the East River yard to Fulton's shop on the New Jersey bank of the Hudson for completion. Coincidentally, the *Fulton the First* was towed over by the commercial steamboat *Fulton*, in company with Robert Fulton's steamboat, the *Car of Neptune*.

Fulton felt very strongly that he needed to personally supervise the completion of his ship. He wrote, "*I cannot trust the construction of the machinery or the fitting out of the* Vessel *to be directed by any one but myself.*"[26] Although the machinery was installed in the ship with no real difficulty, lack of suitable armaments did pose a problem. Guns ultimately had to be transported overland from Philadelphia. Originally, one of Fulton's reasons for developing the steam warship had been to have a vehicle for his submarine guns or "Columbiads." In the transformation of the ship that had since taken place, Fulton had apparently lost interest in his submarine gun and did not develop further this partial prototype of the modern torpedo.

As the fitting out of the *Fulton the First* continued, plans for her future employment were considered. Fulton, no doubt with his late summer visit to Washington and Baltimore in mind, felt that a steam warship would be "important for our Bays and Rivers and the waters leading to Baltimore."[27] Secretary Jones agreed and encouraged a Maryland group to begin planning for a second steam warship at Baltimore. President Madison considered stationing a steam warship on the Great Lakes; however, both Fulton and Stephen Decatur agreed that the ship's engine was not powerful enough to surmount the lakes' occasionally fierce storms and winds. As it turned out, the War of 1812 ended before the *Fulton the First* was ready for action, and the Baltimore project was halted.

The *Fulton the First* was not completed until the summer of 1815, several months after the war had ended with the signing of the "Peace of Christmas Eve" in Europe. The final dimensions of the ship were: length—156 feet, considerably longer than Fulton's original plan; width—56 feet; diameter of wheel—16 feet; and tonnage—2475. Ten minutes after nine on the morning of 4 July 1815, the ship left the pier at Fulton's

The Fulton the First *is launched at New York, 29 October 1814.*
Naval Records and Library

engine works for a trial run to Sandy Hook and back. She accomplished this fifty-three-mile venture into the open sea and back in eight hours and twenty minutes. A passenger reported, "On our arrival at sea, the machinery was stopped, the helm put to starboard, she went about until her head was towards New York when the helm was righted."[28] The ship performed admirably in every respect. About the only problem noted was that it was almost unbearably hot (116°F) in the boiler spaces. The civilian officials reported:

> The Commissioners congratulate the Navy Department and the Nation, on the event of this noble Project, Honourable alike to its Author and its Patrons; It constituted an era in warfare and the arts. The arrival of Peace had indeed disappointed the expectation of conducting her to Battle. That last and conclusive act of shewing her superiority in Combat, it has not been in the power of the Commissioners to make. If a continuance of tranquility should be our lot, and this Steam Vessel of War be not demanded for the Public defence, the Nation has ample cause to rejoice. . . . it becomes the Commissioners to recommend that the Steam Frigate be manned for discipline and practice.[29]

With the war over, the *Fulton the First*'s functions were largely ceremonial. On 18 July 1817, President James Monroe embarked on the ship to visit a friend on Staten Island. European observers were particularly interested in the *Fulton the First*. Both the French and English feared for a time that the great volume of exhaust steam was in reality a new and terrible means of pouring boiling water on defenseless sailors. The British diplomat Stratford Canning observed the ship in 1822 and supported the view that the steam was to be used as a weapon. Apparently, Canning was given conflicting reports about the vessel, one American naval officer telling him that the craft's speed was twelve miles per hour, another saying it was five. Canning noted: " . . . The United States Navy officers seem all to object to her. Notwithstanding the formidable character of this new instrument of war, it is doubtful whether she would be found to answer an adequate purpose in case of actual trial."[30] If this report reflected the true feelings of naval officers in 1822, it would appear that the largely supportive naval attitude of eight years before had greatly changed.

The *Fulton the First* was serving as a receiving ship (processing transient naval personnel) in 1829 when a major explosion took place in her magazine on 4 June. Twenty-four men and one woman were killed, and many others were wounded. Completely destroyed, the first steam warship thus passed into history.

During the fall of 1814, rumors were circulating that William Jones was about to resign as secretary of the Navy. On 5 November 1814, Robert Fulton wrote an unusual letter to President Madison. After having reported on the progress of the steam warship, Fulton predicted that his vessel would bring about "a total revolution in maritime war." He then made an astounding request:

> . . . I will with a frankness which I am certain you
> estimate more highly than any circuitous measures submit to
> your contemplation the means which perhaps may be most
> prompt and efficient for calling into action all the benefits of
> this new system of maritime war. It is reported that Mr.
> Jones intends to resign. If so and I succeed might I not be
> useful in his situation for Twelve months?[31]

Of all Robert Fulton's frank and indeed audacious proposals, this was his boldest. It belies the appraisal of his first biographer, who said of Fulton, "the determination which he often avowed, that he would never accept an office, is an evidence of the disinterestedness of his politics."[32] The designer of the *Fulton the First* was, in fact, the first American inventor to seriously propose himself for a key cabinet post.

Ruth Barlow decided to help Fulton attain his political goal on a woman-to-woman basis. On 12 December 1814, she wrote to the president's wife, Dolley Madison:

> My dear Madam, I am going to take a great liberty with
> you but as my motive is the best, I hope you will have the
> goodness to excuse it, & keep my secret. Have you ever

thought of Mr. Robt. Fulton, as a Man proper (at this time) to fill the Office of Secretary of the Navy? He is an able Engineer his Nautical knowledge is great he has had much practice in Naval Construction, he has energy Integrity, & is devotedly attached to his Country & Government, & his Inventive Genius might perhaps, be made use of, to drive our Savage Invaders from our Coasts which they now so cruelly annoy. This my dear Madm, is only a suggestion to you; should it meet your approbation, & you should speak to the President or Mr. Monroe I pray you, let the Idea come as intirely [sic] from yourself. I would not on any account appear to have thus presumed. & let my motive (which is wholly disinterested) excuse me to you."[33]

Neither the president nor Mrs. Madison's reaction to the above requests are known. President Madison had never been as fond of Fulton as Jefferson had been. Just before leaving office, Secretary of the Navy William Jones submitted to the president a proposal for a major reorganization of the naval department, which, among other things, called for the appointment of a board of naval inspectors and for "the establishment of a Naval Academy."[34] Madison would have received this broad program just after having learned of Fulton's request. Perhaps a partial reason for the president's rejection of Fulton for the top naval post was that Madison did not feel that Fulton had the necessary administrative experience to carry out a program as comprehensive as the one Jones had outlined. If Fulton was not qualified in this respect, President Madison had a man in mind who was. On 24 November, the president wrote to Fulton's old nemesis, Commodore John Rodgers, "The present Secretary of the Navy being about to retire into private life, my thoughts are turned on you for his successor, . . ."[35] Rodgers declined. Madison was apparently quite anxious to find a successor to Jones for he acted in a rather unorthodox fashion. In mid-December, he nominated a prominent Massachusetts merchant named Benjamin Crowninshield for the naval secretaryship, belatedly telling him afterwards, "I hope you will excuse my doing it without your consent which would have been asked, if the business of that Dept. had been less urgent in avoidance of delay."[36] Upon receiving this communication, Crowninshield intended to refuse the post, but when the commission arrived in the mail, he accèpted it. Robert Fulton took this disappointment gracefully and soon established cordial relations with the new appointee. On 16 January 1815, Fulton apprised Crowninshield of all his naval projects. Among other things Fulton proposed "an essay to destroy the British fleet in Kingston [Ontario, Canada] harbor," as well as using the *Fulton the First* "to raise the blockade at New London," upon her scheduled completion in March. Fulton did not know that the Treaty of Ghent had terminated the war three weeks before he wrote to Crowninshield.[37]

Robert Fulton's final months on earth were extremely busy, hectic, and troubled ones. He envisioned a vast steamboat network, not just in the United States but also stretching to Russia

Self-portrait of Robert Fulton. U.S. Naval Institute

and India. He had begun tentative plans for one steamboat to run from St. Petersburg to Kronstadt in Russia and for another to operate between Calcutta and Patna on the Ganges River. During the last year of his life he became increasingly involved in lawsuits and other litigations, usually over patent rights to his steamboats and other inventions. Fulton's fights with his rivals became bitter and virulent. He was particularly angry with two famous architects, William Thornton and Benjamin Latrobe. Of the former, Fulton wrote to Secretary of State James Monroe:

> I regret to trouble you with a very troublesome individual, Dr. Thornton. . . . This is the second time the Doctor has patented my invention. . . . I cannot devote my time and study to my country . . . and see a clerk receiving pay from government permitted to assume my inventions. . . . if he is an inventor a genius who can live by his talents let him do so, but while he is a Clark [*sic*] in the office of the Secretary of State and paid by the public for his services he should be forbid to deal in patents and thereby torment patentees, he should have his choice to quit the office or his pernicious practices. [my god?] Sir I expect this justice of you.[38]

Benjamin Latrobe and Fulton had been friends, but they fell out over western steamboat rivalries on the Ohio River. The friendship was never recovered. One month before Fulton died, he bitterly wrote to Latrobe, "I have your letter of 13th Inst. your letter of details accusing me of all your faults. . . ."[39] Four days later an enraged Fulton assailed another rival inventor, Nathaniel Cutting:

> It is not more than ten minuets [*sic*] I have heared [*sic*] a very extraordinary letter of yours to W. Fairfax read to the house of assembly . . . the whole of which is false and malignant evidently done to injure me and gratify Thornton, Fairfax and other of my sworn enemies. You stated I pirated Cartwright's rope machine and sold it to you, this is untrue. . . . What could induce you to volunteer these falsehoods I cannot conceive. . . . You have stepped forward to be my enemy unprovoked. *I accept it* and will not loose [*sic*] an in-

stant to make you answerable for a libel on my *character as
a man of honor.*[40]

All of these extremely unpleasant encounters occurred just
weeks before Fulton's death and most likely helped hasten his
demise. Is it possible that poet Edgar Lee Masters knew how
close to the truth he was in his poem "Robert Fulton Tanner,"
published in the *Spoon River Anthology* in 1915?

"Robert Fulton Tanner"

If a man could bite the giant hand
That catches and destroys him,
As I was bitten by a rat
While demonstrating my patent trap,
In my hardware store that day.
But a man can never avenge himself
On the monstrous ogre Life.
You enter the room—that's being born;
And then you must live—work out your soul,
Aha! the bait that you crave is in view:
A woman with money you want to marry,
Prestige, place, or power in the world.
But there's work to do and things to conquer—
Oh, yes! the wires that screen the bait.
At last you get in—but you hear a step:
The ogre, Life, comes into the room,
(He was waiting and heard the clang of the spring)
To watch you nibble the wondrous cheese,
And stare with his burning eyes at you,
And scowl and laugh, and mock and curse you,
Running up and down in the trap,
Until your misery bores him.[41]

Although the peace treaty between England and America
had been signed on Christmas Eve, 1814, because of the
slowness of communications, the Battle of New Orleans was
still to take place. In January 1815, General Andrew Jackson
commandeered Fulton's steamboat the *Vesuvius* for standby
duty at New Orleans.[42] In addition, the government paid
Fulton $40,000 to carry American troops down the Ohio and

Mississippi rivers on his steamboats. Ten years after Napoleon
had refused Fulton's offer of his vessels in the invasion of
England, this large sum indicates that the value of Fulton's
steamships as troop transports had finally been recognized.

Robert Fulton's final naval project was the design of a large
semi-submarine craft called the *Mute*. This vessel was to be
eighty feet long and armed with either one submarine gun in
the bow or three on each side. While normally operating on the
surface, it also was to have air chambers which would allow it
to partially submerge if sighted by the enemy. Fulton's 1814
drawing of the *Mute* shows that the ship was to be propelled by
several men turning hand cranks on two shafts, which were attached to a paddlewheel mounted aft amidships. Fulton's arrangement of the crew is reminiscent of slave galleys of old.

Some scholars have confused this vessel with the earlier Long
Island "Turtle Boat," probably because the *Mute* was to be
covered with a protective armored plate. The two boats, however, had two important structural differences. First, the British report on the "turtle boat" describes the deck as "arched
like a turtle shell," while Fulton drew the *Mute* with a flat

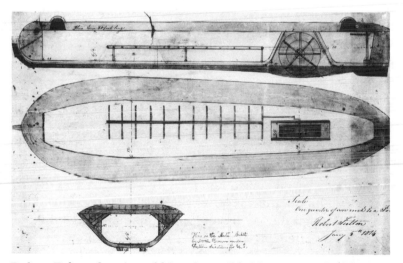

Robert Fulton drawing of his submersible Mute, *1814. Smithsonian Institution*

deck. Secondly, the British officer who destroyed the beached "turtle boat" measured the length of it at twenty-three feet. (See *Mute* drawing.)[43]

According to a note on the drawing (not written by Fulton), Noah Brown built the *Mute* "under Fulton's directions." Although this may have been true, the *Mute* was never fully operational. Fulton did demonstrate a small model to President Madison and other government officials, and he tentatively drew up a plan for her employment. He wrote to Secretary of the Navy Crowninshield:

> . . . Of my last invention of a Bullet Proof boat or *Mute* I have ordered the model from Philadelphia to your office.
> . . . The President will give you his opinion and my plan for rendering this new engine of use, particularly on Lake Ontario where whatever number of ships of war you build, they cannot enter into Kingston harbor to attack the enemy; with the *Mute* I think you can. . . .[44]

Fulton also wrote Madison requesting that several boats of the Mute design be built, ten of these to be constructed at Sackets Harbour on Lake Ontario. The war's end, however, precluded the construction of these vessels. Key naval officers including Rodgers, Chauncey, Porter, and Decatur approved of Fulton's *Mute*, and the acting secretary of the Navy advised Fulton that funds had been appropriated for it. On 17 January, Fulton, temporarily at Trenton, advised Crowninshield that the money for the *Mute* had arrived in New York, adding that, "I will lose no time in executing that work."[45]

Robert Fulton was never able to see his boat built. While at Trenton in January, he was confined to his bed through a combination of fatigue and a cold. Back in New York in February, Fulton and a friend named Emmet were walking across the ice of the Hudson towards the Jersey side one cold day, when Emmet fell through the ice. Fulton pulled him out. According to Fulton's last attending physician: ". . . Mr. Fulton was exceedingly agitated, at the same time that his exertions to save his friend left him very much exhausted: afterwards, con-

Robert Fulton memorial marker, Trinity Church, NY, NY.
Courtesy of Trinity Church, Wall Street, New York, New York

tinuing their walk across the ice, Mr. Fulton became very wet.
. . . When he arrived at his house, he was hoarse, and almost
unable to articulate."[46] Fulton was confined to bed for a few
days but apparently got up before he was completely well. His
throat became reinfected, and the inflammation spread to his
lungs. The doctor was again called for, and he reported:
"Upon approaching his bedside, I at once perceived his situation to be hopeless. The feeble state of his pulse; the hurried
and labored respiration; — his livid and anxious countenance;
— all announced his approaching dissolution. . . . The morning of the succeeding day closed his important life."[47] Robert
Fulton died on 24 February 1815. He left his widow Harriet
and four small children, including one boy named Robert
Barlow Fulton. Many eulogies and honors were accorded him,
but the most fitting tribute to his work in naval warfare came
from Henry Rutgers and the other commissioners of the steam
warship *Fulton the First*. They wrote:

> . . . The world was deprived of his invaluable labours,
> before he had compleated [*sic*] his favorite undertaking. We
> will not enquire, wherefore, in the dispensations of Divine
> Providence, he was not permitted to realise his grand
> conception — But his discoveries survive for the benefit of
> mankind, and will extend to unborn generations.[48]

Robert Fulton
and Naval Warfare

Robert Fulton's work on the submarine, the mine, and the
steam warship represent important contributions to the art of
naval warfare. His secondary inventions, such as the anchor
cutter and the submarine gun, and the use of his steamships to
transport troops, were less significant but still substantial
achievements.

Beginning in 1797, Fulton's work on his naval warfare inventions occupied his life to a much greater degree than did his
work on the more famous steamboat. Only in 1803 and for part
of the 1807-1815 period back in the United States, did the
steamboat share at least equal time with his naval concepts.
Maintaining an active interest in naval warfare until his death
in 1815, Fulton died immersed in the development of two naval
vessels, the *Fulton the First* and the *Mute*.

Fulton himself believed that his work in naval warfare was
more significant than his development of the steamboat. After
the *North River Steam Boat* made its famous voyage up the
Hudson River in 1807, Fulton stated that he did not think it
was "half so important" as his underseas weapons. Thomas Jefferson's substantial correspondence with Robert Fulton indicates that the third president was also more impressed by Fulton's naval weapons than he was by the steamboat.

Both the British and French attempted to duplicate Fulton's
submarine in the latter stages of the Napoleonic wars. During

the American Civil War, the Confederate submarine *Hunley*, modeled in part on Fulton's design, became the first submarine in history to destroy an enemy vessel, a Union ship in Charleston harbor. When John P. Holland, the "father of the modern submarine," tested his *Holland No. 1* on the Passaic River in New Jersey in 1878, he used and further developed the submergence techniques introduced by Fulton. This later inventor also adopted Fulton's ideas on metal construction, the cigar-like shape of the *Nautilus*, the use of a compressed air supply, and the use of two separate means of propulsion for surface and subsurface operations.[1] In 1901, Holland also launched a submarine named *Fulton*. The name of Fulton's original submarine was also used later by others. In 1834 a tract was addressed to senior naval officers calling for reform in the navy; otherwise unidentified, the author used the nom de plume "Nautilus." Fulton's term "Nautilus" was, of course, immortalized by Jules Verne in reference to his submarine in *Twenty Thousand Leagues Under the Sea* in 1870, and in the twentieth century it was the name given to the first atomic submarine.

Robert Fulton's work in mine warfare was part of the basis for the activities of Samuel Colt in the 1840s. According to J.S. Barnes in his then (1869) authoritative *Submarine Warfare*, Fulton wrote in an undated letter to a man named William Brents, Jr. that:

> "Some years ago, I investigated the mode and practicability of firing by electricity under water; the difficulties are, to preserve long wires from being torn or broken — the enemy might float up a few logs or old boats with graplins, [*sic*] and tear away the wires, and thus render the torpedo useless. Another difficulty is to know when the vessel is over the torpedo, for she *must be over it.*"[2]

Colt, best known as inventor of the revolver, also experimented with the electrical detonation of mines and devised an elaborate system of mine warfare. In 1841 Colt wrote a letter to President John Tyler, remarking upon Fulton's book, *Torpedo War and Submarine Explosions*, which had been reprinted in *American State Papers: Naval Affairs* in 1834. Colt told the president that Fulton's book " laid the foundation of my present plan for harbour defense. . . ."[3] The official observer of Colt's system in the Potomac, Colonel Joseph G. Totten, believed, in fact, that Fulton's plan was the better of the two. Writing to the secretary of war in 1844, Totten told him that Fulton's 1807 "torpedo" test in New York harbor had been a "striking success," and that, despite Colt's plans for his own system, Totten believed "any arrangement founded on the principle of Mr. Fulton's anchored torpedoes, presents itself much more favorably to my mind."[4] In 1845 Totten downgraded Colt's system by praising Fulton, "The device of Fulton —is in our opinion far superior to any of its successors—the present one included."[5] In Europe generally, Fulton's mines appear to have had the biggest impact on Russia. While in France, Fulton had presented some of his budding ideas on underwater warfare to General Augustin de Betancourt, who later forwarded the documents to Tsar Alexander I. The Russians liked in particular Fulton's idea of planting stationary mines and during the Crimean War defended Kronstadt with them. An onlooker perhaps overstated the case:

> . . . Russia has brought to perfection Fulton's plans of defence, through the agency of Submarine aids. Millions have been thus directed in the defence of Cronstadt, which place, this day is better defended by Submarine aids than by the immense rock forest with their 6,700 open mouth cannons. . . . 3,740 torpedoes . . . gives a security to the Emperor unknown in the world. These torpedoes the Allies know nothing about.[6]

The great nineteenth-century Russian Admiral Makarov adopted an offensive system including Fulton's spar torpedo on the Danube River during the Russian-Turkish War of 1877–78.[7] In the nineteenth century, the British Admiral "Jacky" Fisher considerably advanced mine warfare through his vigorous support of further research and development of this weapon.[8] Robert Fulton's greatest contribution to modern mine warfare was the invention of the moored mine.

Robert Fulton envisioned a revolution in naval warfare with his concept of transporting troops by steam. His offering his ships to Napoleon for this purpose and the French leader's subsequent rejection would have a greater impact on the twentieth century than Fulton could ever have imagined. In 1939, Enrico Fermi, Edward Teller, and other scientists were discussing the possibilities of nuclear warfare and weapons. They had reached an impasse, however, and needed governmental approval and sanction to continue their work. They therefore sent the scholarly financier Alexander Sachs to seek the support of President Franklin D. Roosevelt. At the first meeting, Sachs spoke at great length and apparently bored Roosevelt with technical details. However, he did receive an invitation to continue the discussion on the following day. During the night Sachs struggled to think of a simple device for communicating the significance of the new weapons. He finally thought of Robert Fulton's attempt to persuade Napoleon to use the steamship to transport his invasion force to England. The next morning President Roosevelt greeted him with "What bright idea have you got now?" Sachs told him of Napoleon's abrupt dismissal of Fulton's scheme, and of his resultant failure. Roosevelt reflected a moment, saw the parallel in the two situations and then called his aide, saying, "This requires action."[9]

Robert Fulton's belief that his submarine and his mines could in the long run secure liberty of the seas and even end war by making it too unpleasant to contemplate was sometimes scoffed at in his day. Our modern age of nuclear weapons, however, has indeed proven true his basic contention that the terrible nature of some weapons can act to deter war.

Finally, the *Fulton the First* was the first steam warship in history. Of particular importance was Fulton's placement of the engine and most of the related machinery below decks, behind the thick walls of the hull. Fulton's concept pre-dated ship designer John Ericsson's *Princeton*, usually considered to be the first steam warship with protected machinery below decks, by almost thirty years. (Ericsson is most famed for his design of the *Monitor* in the Civil War.) Both Britain and France evinced much interest in Fulton's vessel, the British ordering the construction of a somewhat similar ship, the *Congo*, in 1815. The United States Congress authorized the construction of three steam frigates in 1816, but interest died out during the "Era of Good Feelings," and they were never built. Matthew C. Perry, as a young lieutenant, had been greatly impressed by the launching of the *Fulton the First* in October 1814. In 1837, Perry was designated commanding officer of the next steam warship in American history, appropriately named *Fulton the Second*. His support of the steam warship ultimately earned him the nickname, "father of the steam navy."[10] Others experimented with floating steam batteries, but official circles were not greatly impressed.[11] What is striking is the resistance to further development of Fulton's concept prior to the Civil War. Decrying the modern Navy's slowness in building nuclear-powered ships and submarines, Admiral H.G. Rickover, "father of the American Nuclear Navy," wrote in January 1975 of a parallel situation in naval history:

> Changes in the Navy often come at a distressingly slow pace. It took two-thirds of a century for our Navy to change from sail to steam. In 1814, Robert Fulton designed and built for our Navy the world's first warship propelled by steam. It was named *Demologos*. Over the next 20 years the United States built some 700 steam merchantmen while the U.S. Navy built only one steam vessel.[12]

Robert Fulton's weapons and concepts have had an impact on the development of naval warfare that will undoubtedly continue on into the future. His idea that underseas weapons could be used to challenge nations with a superior force of large surface vessels is presently being used by the Soviets, who deploy hundreds of modern submarines throughout all of the world's oceans.

Someone once said that there is nothing so powerful as an idea whose time has come. He might have reversed it and said there is nothing so sad as an idea whose time has not yet come. John Fitch produced a good working steamboat in 1790, but no one cared. That idea's time came in 1807 when Fulton's steamboat chugged up the Hudson. Is it not ironic that Robert Fulton's broad and comprehensive program of naval warfare had to wait until the twentieth century before being carried to fruition?

Notes

PROLOGUE

[1]President Thomas Jefferson, Washington, D.C., to Secretary of War Henry Dearborn, Washington, D.C., 7 July 1807,microfilm reel 62, Thomas Jefferson Mss, Library of Congress.

[2]*Ibid.*

[3]Secretary of War Henry Dearborn, New York, to President Thomas Jefferson, Washington, D.C., 12 July 1807, microfilm reel 62, Thomas Jefferson Mss, Library of Congress.

[4]Secretary of War Henry Dearborn, New York, to Secretary of State James Madison, Washington, D.C., 17 July 1807, microfilm reel 9, James Madison Mss, Library of Congress.

[5]President Thomas Jefferson, Washington, D.C., to Secretary of War Henry Dearborn, New York, 17 July 1807, microfilm reel 63, Thomas Jefferson Mss, Library of Congress.

CHAPTER 1

[1]James T. Lemon, *The Best Poor Man's Country: A Geographical Study of Early Southeastern Pennsylvania,* pp. 7–8.

[2]Robert Fulton, to Joseph Swift and William West, 13 Jan. 1772, item 398, Stauffer Collection, Robert Fulton Mss, Historical Society of Pennsylvania.

[3]Alice Crary Sutcliffe, *Robert Fulton and the Clermont,* pp. 13–14, 21–24.

[4]Robert Fulton Centenary Committee, "Report of the Committee of the Lancaster County Historical Society," p. 216.

[5]Alan Burroughs, *Limners and Likenesses: Three Centuries of American Painting,* p. 111.

[6]Cadwallader D. Colden, *The Life of Robert Fulton,* p. 262.

[7]Joel Barlow, *The Works of Joel Barlow,* 2, p. 708.

[8]Leigh Hunt, *The Autobiography of Leigh Hunt,* 1, p. 100.

[9]Robert Fulton, New York, to Benjamin West, London, 12 July 1813, Box 1A, Robert Fulton Mss, New York Historical Society.

[10]Colden, *The Life of Robert Fulton,* p. 258.

[11]*Ibid.*

[12][M. Strickland] *A Memoir of the Life, Writings, and Mechanical Inventions of Edmund Cartwright,* pp. 134–35.

[13]Colden, *The Life of Robert Fulton,* p. 258.

[14]Robert Fulton, *A Treatise on the Improvement of Canal Navigation,* p. xiii.

[15]Robert Owen, *The Life of Robert Owen Written by Himself,* 1, pp. 65–66.

[16]*Ibid.,* p. 68.

[17]Fulton, *A Treatise on the Improvement of Canal Navigation,* pp. xiii, 2–6, 13.

[18]*Ibid.,* p. xiv.

[19]*Ibid.,* p. 135.

[20]Louis Hartz, *Economic Policy and Democratic Thought: Pennsylvania, 1776–1860* (Chicago: Quadrangle Books, 1968).

[21]John C. Fitzpatrick, ed., *The Writings of George Washington,* 35, pp. 334–35.

[22]Robert Fulton, to Benjamin West, 22 Feb. 1797, Box 1A, Robert Fulton Mss, New York Historical Society.

[23]Owen, *The Life of Robert Owen Written by Himself,* 1, p. 70.

[24]*Ibid.*

[25]*Ibid.*

CHAPTER 2

[1]Robert Fulton, Paris, to the Citizen Directors, Paris, [12 Dec. 1797], reprinted in G.L. Pesce, *La Navigation Sous-Marine,* p. 168.

[2]Reprinted in [M. Strickland] *A Memoir of the Life, Writings, and Mechanical Inventions of Edmund Cartwright,* p 139.

[3]*Ibid.,* p. 140.

[4]Robert Fulton, Paris, to Earl Stanhope, England, 14 Apr. 1798, Montague Collection, Robert Fulton Mss, New York Public Library.

[5]Robert Fulton, Paris, to Joshua Gilpin, London, 20 Nov. 1798, Zabriskie Collection, Robert Fulton Mss, U.S. Naval Academy Museum.

[6]Vincent Nolte, *The Memoirs of Vincent Nolte or Fifty Years in Both Hemispheres* (New York: G. Howard Watt, 1934), p. 180.

[7]Milton Cantor, "A Connecticut Yankee in a Barbary Court: Joel Barlow's Algerian Letters to His Wife," *The William and Mary Quarterly*, 19 (Jan. 1962), p. 97.

[8]Charles Burr Todd, *Life and Letters of Joel Barlow*, p. 294.

[9]Joel Barlow, *The Works of Joel Barlow*, 1, p. 436.

[10]James Woodress, *A Yankee's Odyssey: The Life of Joel Barlow*, p. 215.

[11]Joel Barlow, Paris, to Ruth Barlow, 17 Aug. 1800, reprinted in Todd, *Life and Letters of Joel Barlow*, p. 178.

[12]Reprinted in New York Historical Society, *Official Robert Fulton Exhibition of the Hudson-Fulton Commission*, p. 19.

[13]Robert Fulton, "To the Friends of Mankind," n.d., Box 1B, Robert Fulton Mss, New York Historical Society.

[14]Robert Fulton, "Thoughts on Free Trade," Seligman Collection, Columbia University Library.

[15]Howard Fast, *The Selected Works of Tom Paine and Citizen Tom Paine*, p. 271.

[16]Thomas Paine, *The Complete Writings of Thomas Paine*, ed. Philip S. Foner, 2, pp. 1488-89.

[17]William Barclay Parsons, *Robert Fulton and the Submarine*, pp. 54-55.

[18]Alex Roland, *Underwater Warfare in the Age of Sail*, Ch. 5.

[19]The most persuasive argument in favor of such a meeting is in Alex Roland, *Underwater Warfare in the Age of Sail*, p. 90.

[20]Marie Josephine Louise de Montaut de Navailles, duchess de Gontaut, *Memoirs*, pp. 64-65.

[21]It is difficult to determine from the sources how much Fulton wanted to be paid for the destruction of the British ships. Dickinson states that "400 Livers [*sic*] per gun should be paid for each ship with over forty guns destroyed"; Pesce uses the figure "4000 livres," and Delpeuch uses "4,000 francs." Henry W. Dickinson, *Robert Fulton, Engineer and Artist: His Life and Works*, p. 74; Pesce, *La Navigation Sous-Marine*, p. 168; Maurice Delpeuch, *Les Sous-Marins a travers les siecles*, pp. 75-76.

[22]Pesce, *La Navigation Sous-Marine*, p. 169.

[23]Not 1788 as indicated by Dickinson, *Robert Fulton, Engineer and Artist*, p. 76.

[24]Delpeuch, *Les Sous-Marins a travers les siecles*, pp. 82-83.

[25]Robert Fulton, Paris, to Edmund Cartwright, 16 Feb. 1798, reprinted in [Strickland] *A Memoir of the Life, Writings, and Mechanical Inventions of Edmund Cartwright*, p. 145.

[26]H.F.B. Wheeler and A.M. Broadley, *Napoleon and the Invasion of England*, 1, p. 304.

[27]Robert Fulton, Paris, letter to Joshua Gilpin, London 20 Nov. 1798, Zabriskie Collection, Robert Fulton Mss, U.S. Naval Academy Museum.

[28]Cadwallader D. Colden, *The Life of Robert Fulton*, p. 259.

[29]P.A. Adet, *et al.*, Paris, report to the Minister of Marine, 5 Sept. 1798, reprinted in Pesce, *La Navigation Sous-Marine,* pp. 180-88.

[30]P.A. Adet, *et al.*, Paris, report to the Minister of Marine, 5 Sept. 1798, reprinted in Pesce, *La Navigation Sous-Marine,* p. 187, also Delpeuch, *Les Sous-Marins a travers les siecles,* dedication page.

[31]Pesce, *La Navigation Sous-Marine,* p. 187.

[32]Robert Fulton, to Citizen Director Baras [*sic*], 6 Brumaire An 7 (27 Oct. 1798) Box 1B, Robert Fulton Mss, New York Historical Society.

[33]Robert Fulton, Paris, to Joshua Gilpin, London, 20 Nov. 1798, Zabriskie Collection, Robert Fulton Mss, U.S. Naval Academy Museum.

[34]*Ibid.*

[35]Alan Burroughs, *Limners and Likenesses: Three Centuries of American Painting,* p. 112.

[36]Robert Fulton, Paris, to his mother, 2 July 1799, reprinted in Alice Crary Sutcliffe, *Robert Fulton,* pp. 68-70.

[37]J.S. Cowie, *Mines, Minelayers and Minelaying,* p. 11; Todd, *Life and Letters of Joel Barlow,* p. 177.

[38]P.A.L. Forfait, Paris, to First Consul, Napoleon Bonaparte, 16 June 1800, reprinted in Holden Furber, "Fulton and Napoleon in 1800. New Light on the Submarine Nautilus," p. 492.

[39]Robert Fulton, Paris, to First Consul Napoleon Bonaparte, 15 June 1800, reprinted in Furber, "Fulton and Napoleon in 1800," p. 493.

[40]U.S. Office of Naval Records and Library, *Naval Documents Related to the Quasi War between the United States and France,* 6, p. 470.

[41]Joel Barlow, Paris, to Robert Fulton, 7 Sept. 1800, reprinted in Todd, *Life and Letters of Joel Barlow,* pp. 182-83.

[42]Joel Barlow, Paris, to Ruth Barlow, Le Havre, 31 Aug. 1800, reprinted in Alice Crary Sutcliffe, "Robert Fulton in France," p. 937.

[43]Joel Barlow, Paris, to Ruth Barlow, Le Havre, 4 Sep. 1800, reprinted in Todd, *Life and Letters of Joel Barlow,* p. 181.

[44]Robert Fulton, Paris, to Minister of Marine, 3 Dec. 1800, reprinted in Pesce, *La Navigation Sous-Marine,* p. 205.

[45]J. Dumaine and Henri Plon, eds., *Correspondence de Napoleon Ier,* 6, p. 522.

[46]Robert Fulton, Paris, to Citizens Monge, Laplace, and Volney, 9 Sep. 1801, reprinted in Sutcliffe, "Robert Fulton in France," p. 940.

[47]Joseph Farington, *The Farington Diary,* ed. James Greig, 2, p. 103.

[48]Robert Fulton, Paris, to Citizens Monge, Laplace, and Volney, 9 Sep. 1801, reprinted in Sutcliffe, "Robert Fulton in France," p. 941.

[49]Robert Fulton, Paris, to Edmund Cartwright, 28 Mar. 1802, reprinted in [Strickland] *A Memoir of the Life, Writings, and Mechanical Inventions of Edmund Cartwright,* pp. 154-56.

[50]Robert Fulton, to Citizens Monge, Laplace, and Volney, 20 Sep. 1801, reprinted in Sutcliffe, "Robert Fulton in France," p. 939.

[51]*Ibid.,* pp. 939-40.

[52]Robert Fulton, New York, to Messrs. Volney, Monge, and La Place, Paris, 12 Mar. 1810, Montague Collection, Robert Fulton Mss, New York Public Library.

[53]Pesce, *La Navigation Sous-Marine*, p. 208.

[54]Joel Barlow, Paris, to Robert Fulton, 14 June 1802, reprinted in Todd, *Life and Letters of Joel Barlow*, p. 190.

[55]Israel Thrask, Paris, to his wife, 12 Oct. 1800, reprinted in U.S. Office of Naval Records and Library, *Naval Documents Related to the Quasi-War between the United States and France*, 6, pp. 470-71.

[56]M. Bourrienne, *Memoirs of Napoleon Bonaparte*, 2, p. 43.

[57]J. Christopher Herold, ed., *The Mind of Napoleon: A Selection from His Written and Spoken Words*, trans. J. Christopher Herold, p. 70.

[58]Pesce, *La Navigation Sous-Marine*, p. 227.

[59]"The First Submarine Boat," *Scientific American Supplement*, p. 2.

[60]Joel Barlow, Paris, to Ruth Barlow, 1 May 1802, reprinted in Todd, *Life and Letters of Joel Barlow*, pp. 184-85.

[61]John Fitch, Philadelphia, to Richard Wells, 13 Jul. 1792, Vol. 147, "Inventors," Dreer Collection, Historical Society of Pennsylvania.

[62]Thomas Jefferson, Monticello, to Dr. Benjamin Waterhouse, 3 Mar. 1818, reprinted in Adrienne Koch and William Peden, eds., *The Life and Selected Writings of Thomas Jefferson*, p. 686.

[63]Ghita Stanhope and G.P. Gooch, *The Life of Charles Third Earl Stanhope*, p. 174.

[64][Strickland] *A Memoir of the Life, Writings, and Mechanical Inventions of Edmund Cartwright*, pp. 133-61.

[65]Robert Fulton, Paris, to Edmund Cartwright, 20 Sep. 1797, reprinted in [Strickland] *A Memoir of the Life, Writings and Mechanical Inventions of Edmund Cartwright*, p. 141.

[66]Robert R. Livingston, Paris, to Thomas Tillotson, 12 Nov. 1802, Miscellaneous manuscripts, Robert R. Livingston Mss, New York Historical Society.

[67]George Dangerfield, *Chancellor Robert R. Livingston of New York 1746 -1813*, pp. 403-422.

[68]Robert Fulton, Paris, letter to Fulmer Skipwith, 20 Sep. 1802, Case 7, Gratz Collection, Robert Fulton Mss, Historical Society of Pennsylvania.

[69]Germaine, Baroness de Stael-Holstein, *Ten Years Exile*, ed. Augustus, Baron de Stael-Holstein, p. 85.

[70]Edouard Desbriere, *Projets et tentatives de debarquement aux îles Britanniques*, 3, p. 308.

[71]D.A. Bingham, ed., *A Selection from the Letters and Despatches of the First Napoleon* (London: Chapman & Hall, 1884), 2, p. 38.

[72]Etienne-Denis Duc Pasquier, *A History of My Time: Memoirs of Chancellor Pasquier*, ed. the Duc d'Audiffret-Pasquier; trans. Charles E. Roche, 1, pp. 177-78.

[73]U.S. Congress, *American State Papers: Foreign Affairs*, 2, p. 525.
[74]Desbriere, *Projets et tentatives de debarquement aux iles Britanniques*, 3, p. 312.

CHAPTER 3

[1]Joshua Gilpin, London, to Lord Stanhope, 28 Aug. 1798, reprinted in Alice Crary Sutcliffe, "Robert Fulton in France," p. 935.

[2]Joel Barlow, Paris, to Robert Fulton, 21 May 1802, reprinted in Charles Burr Todd, *Life and Letters of Joel Barlow*, pp. 186–87.

[3]Joseph Farington, *The Farington Diary*, ed. James Greig, 2, p. 102.

[4]Evan Nepean, Admiralty Office, London, secret circular to Admirals Lord Keith, Montagu, Cornwallis, Colpoys, 19 June 1803, Montague Collection, Robert Fulton Mss, New York Public Library.

[5]Alice Crary Sutcliffe, *Robert Fulton*, p. 104; Robert Fulton, "Motives for inventing Submarine Navigation and attack," in William Barclay Parsons, *Robert Fulton and the Submarine*, p. 55.

[6]Robert Fulton, Amsterdam, to Daniel Parker (Paris?), 27 Oct. 1803, Box 1A, Robert Fulton Mss, New York Historical Society.

[7]"Letters and Documents by or Relating to Robert Fulton," *New York Public Library Bulletin*, p. 569.

[8]Fulton, "Motives for inventing Submarine Navigation and attack," in Parsons, *Robert Fulton and the Submarine*, p. 59.

[9]Bradford Perkins, *Prologue to War: England and the United States, 1805–1812* (Berkeley and Los Angeles: University of California Press, 1968), p. 13.

[10]Lord Castlereagh, London, "Most Secret" letter to Lord Barham, 20 Oct. 1805, State Department Preliminary Inventories, E-807 (Fulton Papers), Record Group 59, National Archives.

[11]Robert Francis (Fulton), London, proposals (to the Pitt ministry), 22 May 1804, Montague Collection, Robert Fulton Mss, New York Public Library.

[12]Henry W. Dickinson, *Robert Fulton, Engineer and Artist*, p. 166; Parsons, *Robert Fulton and the Submarine*, pp. 85–86.

[13]Reprinted in Parsons, *Robert Fulton and the Submarine*, p. 102.

[14]*The Farington Diary*, 3, p. 164.

[15]Robert Fulton, New York, agreement with William Lee, 22 May 1811, Personnel (Misc.), Box 23, Robert Fulton Mss, New York Public Library.

[16]p. 45.

[17]"Messenger" drawing, n.d., item number 1855.18.3, Vol. 4, Solomon Alofsen Collection, Robert Fulton Mss, New Jersey Historical Society.

[18]W.G. Perrin, ed., *The Keith Papers*, 3, p. 7.

[19]Robert Fulton, Storeys Gate Coffeehouse, to William Pitt, 6 June 1804,

reprinted in Parsons, *Robert Fulton and the Submarine*, p. 96.

²⁰Robert Fulton, Storeys Gate Coffeehouse, London, to Mr. Hammond, 22 June 1804, Montague Collection, Robert Fulton Mss, New York Public Library.

²¹Marie Josephine Louise de Montaut de Navailles, duchesse de Gontaut, *Memoirs*, pp. 130-31.

²²William Pitt and Lord Melville, contract with Robert Fulton, 20 July 1804, Montague Collection, Robert Fulton Mss, New York Public Library.

²³D.A. Bingham, ed., *A Selection from the Letters and Despatches of the First Napoleon* (London: Chapman & Hall, 1884), 2, p. 83.

²⁴Perrin, ed., *The Keith Papers*, 3, p. 88.

²⁵*Ibid.*, pp. 92-93.

²⁶Letter, 3 Oct. 1804, reprinted in H.F.B Wheeler and A.M. Broadly, *Napoleon and the Invasion of England*, 1, pp. 313-14.

²⁷Alexander Allardyce, *Memoir of the Honourable George Keith Elphinstone*, p. 345.

²⁸U.S. Congress, *American State Papers: Naval Affairs*, 1, p. 216.

²⁹Perrin, ed., *The Keith Papers*, 3, p. 95.

³⁰Sir Evan Nepean, Dublin Castle, to John King, 9 Oct. 1804, reprinted in Wheeler and Broadly, *Napoleon and the Invasion of England*, 1, pp. 314-15.

³¹Perrin, ed., *The Keith Papers*, 3, p. 95.

³²*Ibid.*, p. 101.

³³Robert Stewart, Viscount Castlereagh, *Correspondence, Despatches, and Other Papers*, ed. Charles William Vane, Marquess of Londonderry, 5, pp. 86-87.

³⁴*Ibid.*, pp. 91-94.

³⁵Rear Admiral La Crosse, Boulogne, to Minister of Marine, 1 Oct. 1805, reprinted in Henry Harrison Suplee, "Fulton in France," p. 418.

³⁶A. Crawford, *Reminiscences of a Naval Officer during the Late War*, 1, p. 128.

³⁷U.S. Congress, *American State Papers: Naval Affairs*, 1, p. 217.

³⁸Robert Fulton, Dover, to "Mamy" West, 16 Oct. 1805, Box 1A, Robert Fulton Mss, New York Historical Society.

³⁹U.S. Congress, *American State Papers: Naval Affairs*, 1, p. 212; Castlereagh, *Correspondence, Despatches, and Other Papers*, 5, pp. 119-20.

⁴⁰Robert Fulton, Dover, to "Mamy" West, 16 Oct. 1805, Box 1A, Robert Fulton Mss, New York Historical Society; and U.S. Congress, *American State Papers: Naval Affairs*, 1, p. 212.

⁴¹Robert Fulton, Dover, to "Mamy" West, 16 Oct. 1805, Box 1A, Robert Fulton Mss, New York Historical Society.

⁴²Lord Castlereagh, London, "Most Secret" letter to Lord Barham, 20 Oct. 1805, State Department Preliminary Inventories, E-807 (Fulton Papers), Record Group 59, National Archives.

⁴³Robert Fulton, London, to his sister, 20 Oct. 1805, Montague Collec-

tion, Robert Fulton Mss, New York Public Library.

⁴⁴Castlereagh, *Correspondence, Despatches, and Other Papers*, 5, pp. 124-25.

⁴⁵U.S. Congress, *American State Papers: Naval Affairs*, 1, p. 213.

⁴⁶Robert Fulton, Dover, to "Mamy" West, 16 Oct. 1805, Box 1A, Robert Fulton Mss, New York Historical Society.

⁴⁷U.S. Congress, *American State Papers: Naval Affairs*, 1, p. 223.

⁴⁸Crawford, *Reminiscences of a Naval Officer during the Late War*, 1, pp. 128-29.

⁴⁹Admiral George Berkeley, Halifax, Nova Scotia, to James Barry, 14 Sep. 1807, Case 4, Box 36, Gratz Collection, Robert Fulton Mss, Historical Society of Pennsylvania.

⁵⁰Castlereagh, *Correspondence, Despatches, and Other Papers*, 5, p. 131.

⁵¹*Ibid.*, p. 132.

⁵²Stanislaus Murray Hamilton, ed., *The Writings of James Monroe*, 4, p.373.

⁵³Robert Fulton, London, to William Pitt, 6 Jan. 1806, State Department Preliminary Inventories, F-807 (Fulton Papers), Record Group 59, National Archives.

⁵⁴*Ibid.*

⁵⁵Joel Barlow, Washington, D.C., to Robert Fulton, 3 Mar. 1806, reprinted in Sutcliffe, *Robert Fulton and the Clermont*, pp. 168-70; James Woodress, *A Yankee's Odyssey: The Life of Joel Barlow*, p. 244.

⁵⁶Arbitrators' Report, London, 5 Aug. 1806, State Department Preliminary Inventories, F-807 (Fulton Papers), Record Group 59, National Archives.

⁵⁷Reprinted in Alice Crary Sutcliffe, "The Early Life of Robert Fulton," p. 781.

CHAPTER 4

¹*National Intelligencer and Washington Advertiser*, 22 Dec. 1806, p. 3.

²Joel Barlow, Washington, D.C., to Stephen Barlow, 15 Dec. 1807, quoted in Allen C. Clark, *Life and Letters of Dolley Madison* (Washington, D.C.: W.F. Roberts., 1914), pp. 444-45.

³Fred A. Emery, "Washington's Historic Bridges," pp. 62 63.

⁴*National Intelligencer and Washington Advertiser*, 16 Jan. 1807, pp. 2-3.

⁵"Robert Fulton's Torpedoes," *Scientific American*, p. 361.

⁶Reprinted in *National Intelligencer and Washington Advertiser*, 24 July 1807, p. 3.

⁷Robert Fulton, New York, to President Thomas Jefferson, Washington, D.C., 28 July 1807, microfilm reel 63, Thomas Jefferson Mss, Library of Congress.

⁸U.S. Congress, *American State Papers: Naval Affairs*, 1, p. 213.

[9]Robert Fulton, New York, to President Thomas Jefferson, Washington, D.C., 28 July 1807, microfilm reel 63, Thomas Jefferson Mss, Library of Congress.

[10]E. Millicent Sowerby, ed., *Catalogue of the Library of Thomas Jefferson*, 1, p. 526.

[11]Robert Fulton, London, to President Thomas Jefferson, Washington, D.C., 23 May 1804, microfilm reel 48, Thomas Jefferson Mss, Library of Congress.

[12]President Thomas Jefferson, Monticello, to Robert Fulton, New York, 16 Aug. 1807, microfilm reel 63, Thomas Jefferson Mss, Library of Congress.

[13]*Ibid.*

[14]Andrew A. Lipscomb and Albert E. Bergh, eds., *The Writings of Thomas Jefferson*, 11, pp. 336–37.

[15]Catherine Mitchill, New York, to Margaret Miller, New York, 17 Aug. 1807, Society Autograph Collection, Robert Fulton Mss, Historical Society of Pennsylvania.

[16]Donald C. Ringwald, "First Steamboat to Albany," p. 159; Cedric Ridgely-Nevitt, "The Steam Boat, 1807–1814," p. 27.

[17]Charles Burr Todd, *Life and Letters of Joel Barlow*, pp. 233–34; J. Munsell, "Steam Navigation on the Hudson," pp. 20–22; "Robert Fulton's First Voyage," *Hunt's Merchant Magazine*, 15 (Nov. 1846), p. 471.

[18]George Dangerfield, *Chancellor Robert R. Livingston of New York 1746–1813*, p. 409.

[19]Benjamin West, London, to Robert Fulton, 23 Sep. 1808, Zabriskie Collection, Robert Fulton Mss, U.S. Naval Academy Museum.

[20]Robert Fulton, New York, to Captain Brink, 9 Oct. 1807, reprinted in Thomas S. Clarkson, *A Biographical History of Clermont or Livingston Manor*, p. 139.

[21]Robert Fulton, Washington, D.C., to President Thomas Jefferson, Washington, D.C., 3 Dec. 1807, microfilm reel 65, Thomas Jefferson Mss, Library of Congress.

[22]Robert Fulton, Belair, Maryland, to President Thomas Jefferson, Washington, D.C., 9 Dec. 1807, microfilm reel 65, Thomas Jefferson Mss, Library of Congress.

[23]Joel Barlow, Belair, Maryland, to President Thomas Jefferson, Washington, D.C., 9 Dec. 1807, microfilm reel 65, Thomas Jefferson Mss, Library of Congress.

[24]President Thomas Jefferson, Washington, D.C., letters to Robert Fulton and Joel Barlow, Belair, Maryland, 10 Dec. 1807, microfilm reel 65, Thomas Jefferson Mss, Library of Congress.

[25]Robert Fulton, Washington, D.C., to President Thomas Jefferson, Monticello, 5 Aug. 1808, microfilm reel 68, Thomas Jefferson Mss, Library of Congress.

[26]President Thomas Jefferson, Monticello, to Secretary of the Navy Robert Smith, Washington, D.C., 12 Aug. 1808, microfilm reel 68, Thomas Jefferson Mss, Library of Congress.

[27]H.A. Washington, ed., *The Writings of Thomas Jefferson*, 5, p. 342.

[28]Robert Fulton, Kalorama, Washington, D.C., to President Thomas Jefferson, Washington, D.C., 24 Jan. 1809, microfilm reel 71, Thomas Jefferson Mss, Library of Congress.

[29]Robert Fulton, Kalorama, Washington, D.C., to President-elect James Madison, Washington, D.C., 28 Jan. 1809, microfilm reel 10, James Madison Mss, Library of Congress.

[30]Robert Fulton, Kalorama, Washington, D.C., to President-elect James Madison, Washington, D.C., 9 Feb. 1809, microfilm reel 10, James Madison Mss, Library of Congress.

[31]Robert Fulton, Bush Inn, to President-elect James Madison, Washington, D.C., 17 Feb. 1809, microfilm reel 10, James Madison Mss, Library of Congress.

[32]Robert Fulton, Bush Inn, to President-elect James Madison, Washington, D.C., 17 Feb. 1809, microfilm reel 10, James Madison Mss, Library of Congress.

[33]Irving Brant, *James Madison: The President, 1809–1812*, pp. 336, 438–39; Samuel Eliot Morison, *"Old Bruin" Commodore Matthew C. Perry 1794–1858*, p. 30; Leonard D. White, *The Jeffersonians*, pp. 80, 271.

[34][Joel Barlow] *The Works of Joel Barlow*, 1, pp. 535–36. Note that Barlow's words, "submarine attack," refer to the underwater nature of Fulton's mine warfare, not to the submarine itself.

[35]Robert Fulton, New York, to Robert R. Livingston, Clermont, 27 Dec. 1809, Miscellaneous manuscripts, Robert R. Livingston Mss, New York Historical Society.

[36]Robert Fulton, *Concluding Address on the Mechanism, Practice and Effects of Torpedoes*, pp. 9–10.

[37]Secretary of the Navy Paul Hamilton, Washington, D.C., to Commodore John Rodgers, New York, 22 Feb. 1810, microfilm reel 1 of Mr. Frederick Rodgers's collection of John Rodgers's papers, New York Historical Society.

[38]See Charles Oscar Paullin, *Commodore John Rodgers, Captain, Commodore, and Senior Officer of the American Navy, 1773–1838*.

[39]C.W. Goldsborough, Washington, D.C., to Commodore John Rodgers, New York, 24 Feb. 1810, microfilm reel 1 of Mr. Frederick Rodgers's collection of John Rodgers's papers, New York Historical Society.

[40]Robert Fulton, Kalorama, Washington, D.C., to Thomas Jefferson, Monticello, 24 Feb. 1810, microfilm reel 73, Thomas Jefferson Mss, Library of Congress.

[41]Robert Fulton, New York, to R. Bradley, Washington, D.C., 5 Mar. 1810, Box 1A, Robert Fulton Mss, New York Historical Society.

[42]Commodore John Rodgers, to his wife, 13 Mar. 1810, microfilm reel 1 of Mr. Frederick Rodgers's collection of John Rodgers's papers, New York Historical Society.

[43]Thomas Jefferson, Monticello, to Robert Fulton, New York, 17 Mar. 1810, microfilm reel 73, Thomas Jefferson Mss, Library of Congress.

[44]Thomas Jefferson, Monticello, to Robert Fulton, New York, 16 Apr. 1810, microfilm reel 73, Thomas Jefferson Mss, Library of Congress.

[45]Secretary of the Navy Paul Hamilton, Washington, D.C., to Robert Fulton, New York, 30 Mar. 1810, Vol. 10, p. 170, M 209/4, Record Group 45, Navy Department Library.

[46]Robert Fulton, New York, to Secretary of the Navy Paul Hamilton, Washington, D.C., 3 May 1810, Montague Collection, Robert Fulton Mss, New York Public Library.

[47]Secretary of the Navy Paul Hamilton, Washington, letters to Oliver Wolcott, Cadwallader Colden, Chancellor Robert R. Livingston, Governor Morgan Lewis, "Col. Williams, Mr. Garnet and Doc. Kemp," New York, 4 May 1810, Vol. 10, p. 191, and to Robert Fulton, New York, Vol. 10, pp. 192-93, M 209/4, Record Group 45, Navy Department Library.

[48]Robert Fulton, New York, to Secretary of the Navy Paul Hamilton, Washington, D.C., 9 May 1810, Box 1A, Robert Fulton Mss, New York Historical Society.

[49]See Vol. 10, M 209/4, Record Group 45, Navy Department Library.

[50]U.S. Congress, *American State Papers: Naval Affairs*, 1, p. 243.

[51]*Ibid.*, p. 241.

[52]*Ibid.*, p. 235.

[53]Robert Fulton, to unknown addressee, appended to "A Citizen of Philadelphia 8 Dec. 1807, [author]," *The Second Crisis for America* (New York: John H. Sherman, 1815), pp. 85-87.

[54]Perry Miller, *The Life of the Mind in America: From the Revolution to the Civil War*, p. 302.

[55]Quoted in Avrahm Yarmolinsky, *Picturesque United States of America: A Memoir on Paul Svinin*, pp. 9-10.

[56]"Letters and Documents by or relating to Robert Fulton," *New York Public Library Bulletin*, p. 579.

[57]James F. Hopkins, ed., *The Papers of Henry Clay* (Lexington: University of Kentucky Press, 1961), 2, p. 459.

[58]Robert Fulton, New York, to "Messrs. Volney, Mange [sic], and La Place," Paris, 12 Mar. 1810, Montague Collection, Robert Fulton Mss, Public Library.

[59]Robert Fulton, New York, to Earl Stanhope, 3 Apr. 1810, Montague Collection, Robert Fulton Mss, New York Public Library.

[60]U.S. Congress, *American State Papers: Naval Affairs*, 1, p. 222.

[61]See Edward K. Eckert, "William Jones: Mr. Madison's Secretary of the Navy," and "Early Reform in the Navy Department," pp. 231, 245; Ken-

neth L. Brown, "Mr. Madison's Secretary of the Navy;" White, *The Jeffersonians*, pp. 271–73.

[62]Robert Fulton, New York, to Commodore Jacob Lewis, 26 Jan. 1814, Vol. 168, pp. 35–36, Dreer Collection, Robert Fulton Mss, Historical Society of Pennsylvania.

[63]Thomas Jefferson, Monticello, to Robert Fulton, New York, 8 Mar. 1813, microfilm reel 77, Thomas Jefferson Mss, Library of Congress.

[64]Robert Fulton, New York, "Notes on the practice of Torpedoes," 26 Mar. 1813, Zabriskie Collection, Robert Fulton Mss, U.S. Naval Academy Museum.

[65]Robert Fulton, New York, to Secretary of State James Monroe, Washington, D.C., 4 May 1813, Zabriskie Collection, Robert Fulton Mss, U.S. Naval Academy Museum.

[66]Robert Fulton, to William Brents, Jr., Aquia, Virginia, n.d., quoted in J.S. Barnes, *Submarine Warfare,* pp. 229–30.

[67]Robert Fulton, New York, to Robert R. Livingston, 24 Sep. 1812, Miscellaneous manuscripts, Robert R. Livingston Mss, New York Historical Society.

[68]Thomas Jefferson, Monticello, to Robert Fulton, New York, 8 Mar 1813, microfilm reel 77, Thomas Jefferson Mss, Library of Congress.

[69]"Torpedoes and Diving Boats," *Niles Weekly Register*, 4 (7 Aug. 1813), p. 365.

[70]Philip K. Lundeberg, *Samuel Colt's Submarine Battery: The Secret and the Enigma*, p. 22.

[71]William L. Calderhead, "Naval Innovation in Crisis: War in the Chesapeake, 1813," p. 216.

[72]Talbot Hamlin, *Benjamin Henry Latrobe*, pp. 390–91.

[73]*Niles Weekly Register*, 4 (17 July 1813), pp. 326–27.

[74]Captain Thomas Hardy, HMS *Ramilies* off New London, to Major Ben. Case, Sag Harbor, Long Island, New York, 23 Aug. 1813, reprinted in *Niles Weekly Register*, 5 (11 Sep. 1813), pp. 27–28.

[75]See especially W.B. Rowbotham, "Robert Fulton's Turtle Boat," pp. 1,716–19.

[76]See George Hagerman, "Lord of the Turtle Boats," pp. 66–75.

[77]*Niles Weekly Register*, 6 (9 July 1814), p. 318.

[78]Robert Fulton, memorandum, n.d., Montague Collection, Robert Fulton Mss, New York Public Library.

[79]Stephen Decatur, New York, statement, 6 May 1813, microfilm reel 77, Thomas Jefferson Mss, Library of Congress.

[80]Hanson W. Baldwin, "Fulton and Decatur: An Unpublished Document," pp. 231–35.

[81]Sowerby, ed., *Catalogue of the Library of Thomas Jefferson*, I, p. 526.

[82]Robert Fulton, New York, letters to Stephen Decatur, New London, 5 Aug., 4 Sep., and 12 Sep. 1813, Zabriskie Collection, Robert Fulton Mss, U.S. Naval Academy Museum.

[83]Robert Fulton, "Diary," 8-9 Sep. 1814, Montague Collection, Robert Fulton Mss, New York Public Library.

[84]Robert Fulton, New York, to Commodore John Rodgers, Baltimore, 14 Sep. 1814, Montague Collection, Robert Fulton Mss, New York Public Library.

CHAPTER 5

[1]Robert Fulton, New York, to Thomas Jefferson, Monticello, 8 July 1813, microfilm reel 77, Thomas Jefferson Mss, Library of Congress.

[2]Robert Fulton, New York, to Commodore Stephen Decatur, New London, 5 Aug. 1813, Zabriskie Collection, Robert Fulton Mss, U.S. Naval Academy Museum.

[3]Stephen Decatur, New London, to Robert Fulton, New York, 3 Aug. 1813, General Manuscript Collection, U.S. Naval Academy Museum.

[4]Ralph Gurley, USS Fulton the First, p. 325 and Tyler, American Neptune, p. 257.

[5]Robert Fulton, "Sketches," November 1813, reprinted in David B. Tyler, "Fulton's Steam Frigate," pp. 255-56.

[6]Ibid., pp. 253-54.

[7]Robert Fulton Papers, Vol. 168, p. 6, Dreer Collection, Robert Fulton Mss, Historical Society of Pennsylvania.

[8]Stephen Decatur, New London, to Robert Fulton, New York, 31 Dec. 1813, Vol. 168. pp. 12-13, Dreer Collection, Robert Fulton Mss, Historical Society of Pennsylvania.

[9]Stephen Decatur, J. Jones, and J. Biddle, New London, 3 Jan. 1814, and Samuel Evans, O.H. Perry, L. Warrington, and J. Lewis, New York, 10 Jan. 1814, certificate "Steam Vessel of War," Box 1B, Robert Fulton Mss, New York Historical Society.

[10]Robert Fulton, New York, to Secretary of the Navy William Jones, Washington, D.C., 14 Jan. 1814, certificate "Steam Vessel of War," Box 1B, Robert Fulton Mss, New York Historical Society.

[11]Robert Fulton, New York, to Secretary of State James Munroe [sic], 4 Jan. 1814, Vol. 168, p. 32, Dreer Collection, Robert Fulton Mss, Historical Society of Pennsylvania.

[12]Certificate "Steam Vessel of War," Box 1B, Robert Fulton Mss, New York Historical Society.

[13]Henry Clay, Washington, D.C., to Robert Fulton, New York, 27 Jan. 1814, Vol. 168, pp. 14-15, Dreer Collection, Robert Fulton Mss, Historical Society of Pennsylvania.

[14]Robert Fulton, New York, to Commodore Oliver Hazard Perry, Washington, D.C., 26 Jan. 1814, Montague Collection, Robert Fulton Mss, New York Public Library.

[15]Secretary of the Navy William Jones, Washington, D.C., to Chairman of House Naval Committee William Lowndes, Washington, D.C., 2 Feb.

1814, reprinted in *Documents Relating to the Claims of the Heirs of Robert Fulton*, p. 17.

[16]Robert Fulton, Albany, to President James Madison, Washington, D.C., 23 Mar. 1814, microfilm reel 16, James Madison Mss, Library of Congress.

[17]Secretary of the Navy William Jones, Washington, D.C., to Robert Fulton, New York, 6 May 1814, Vol. 12, pp. 158-60, M 209/4, Record Group 45, Navy Department Library.

[18]Adam and Noah Brown, New York, to Robert Fulton, New York, 16 May 1814, Vol. 168, pp. 74-75, Dreer Collection, Robert Fulton Mss, Historical Society of Pennsylvania.

[19]Robert Fulton, memorandum "Steam Floating Batteries," spring 1814, Box 1A, Robert Fulton Mss, New York Historical Society.

[20]See Howard I. Chapelle, *Fulton's "Steam Battery": Blockship and Catamaran*.

[21]Henry Rutgers, New York, to Secretary of the Navy William Jones, Washington, D.C., 30 Aug. 1814, Vol. 168, pp. 136-37, Dreer Collection, Robert Fulton Mss, Historical Society of Pennsylvania.

[22]Robert Fulton, Baltimore, to President James Madison, Washington, D.C., 8 Sep. 1814, Vol. 168, p. 140, Dreer Collection, Robert Fulton Mss, Historical Society of Pennsylvania.

[23]Robert Fulton, "Diary," 3-4 Sep. 1814, Montague Collection, Robert Fulton Mss, New York Public Library.

[24]Secretary of the Navy William Jones, Washington, D.C., to Captain David Porter, 8 Sep. 1814, Vol. 168, pp. 141-42, Dreer Collection, Robert Fulton Mss, Historical Society of Pennsylvania.

[25]David Porter, New York, to Secretary of the Navy William Jones, Washington, D.C., 29 Oct. 1814, Vol. 168, pp. 154-55, Dreer Collection, Robert Fulton Mss, Historical Society of Pennsylvania.

[26]Robert Fulton, New York, to General Jonathan Williams, Philadelphia, 23 Nov. 1814, New York Public Library, "Letters and Documents by or Relating to Robert Fulton," p. 580.

[27]Robert Fulton, New York, to Josiah Ogden, 9 Nov. 1814, Box 1B, Robert Fulton Mss, New York Historical Society.

[28]["A Nautical Gentleman on board"], "Cruise of the steam frigate Fulton the First," 4 July 1815, Vol. 160, pp. 106-00, Dreer Collection, Robert Fulton Mss, Historical Society of Pennsylvania.

[29]Henry Rutgers, Samuel L. Mitchill, Thomas Morris, "Report of the Commissioners superintending the Construction of a Steam Vessel of War," 28 Dec. 1815, Montague Collection, Robert Fulton Mss, New York Public Library.

[30]Stratford Canning, 1822, "Notes on Steam Frigate," reprinted in Arthur J. May, "Stratford Canning on Shipping in America," *American Neptune*, 4 (Oct. 1944), p. 328.

[31]Robert Fulton, New York, to President James Madison, Washington,

D.C., 5 Nov. 1814, microfilm reel 16, James Madison Mss, Library of Congress.

[32]Cadwallader D. Colden, *The Life of Robert Fulton*, p. 259.

[33]Mrs. Joel Barlow, to Dolley Madison, Washington, D.C., 12 Dec. 1814, letter in collection, Robert A. Rutland, editor in chief, *The Papers of James Madison*.

[34]Secretary of the Navy William Jones, Washington, D.C., to the President of the Senate, Washington, D.C., 15 Nov. 1814, microfilm reel 16, James Madison Mss, Library of Congress.

[35]President James Madison, Washington, D.C., to Commodore John Rodgers, 24 Nov. 1814, microfilm reel 16, James Madison Mss, Library of Congress.

[36]President James Madison, Washington, D.C., to Benjamin Crowninshield, 15 Dec. 1814, microfilm reel 16, James Madison Mss, Library of Congress.

[37]Robert Fulton, Trenton, to Secretary of the Navy Benjamin Crowninshield, Washington, D.C., 16 Jan. 1815, Vol. 168, p. 183, Dreer Collection, Robert Fulton Mss, Historical Society of Pennsylvania.

[38]Robert Fulton, Washington, D.C., to Secretary of War [and State] James Monroe, 27 Dec. 1814, Zabriskie Collection, Robert Fulton Mss, U.S. Naval Academy Museum.

[39]Robert Fulton, New York, to Benjamin Latrobe, 24 Jan. 1815, Montague Collection, Robert Fulton Mss, New York Public Library.

[40]Robert Fulton, Trenton, to Nathaniel Cutting, Washington, D.C., 28 Jan. 1815, Montague Collection, Robert Fulton Mss, New York Public Library.

[41]Edgar Lee Masters, *Spoon River Anthology* (New York: Collier Books, 1962), p. 28.

[42]Third Auditor's Office, to Robert Fulton's estate representatives, 15 May 1820, Miscellaneous Letters Sent, Vol. 16, Record Group 217, General Accounting Office, National Archives; *Documents Relating to the Claims of the Heirs of Robert Fulton*, pp. 6-7, 20-23.

[43]W.B. Rowbotham, "Robert Fulton's Turtle Boat," pp. 1,746-47.

[44]Robert Fulton, Trenton, letter to Secretary of the Navy Benjamin Crowninshield, Washington, D.C., 16 Jan. 1815, Vol. 168, pp. 184-86, Dreer Collection, Robert Fulton Mss, Historical Society of Pennsylvania.

[45]Robert Fulton, Trenton, to Secretary of the Navy Benjamin Crowninshield, Washington, D.C., 17 Jan. 1815, Vol. 168, p. 187, Dreer Collection, Robert Fulton Mss, Historical Society of Pennsylvania.

[46]Dr. David Hosack, New York, to Cadwallader Colden, 1 Jan. 1817, reprinted in Colden, *The Life of Robert Fulton*, p. 266.

[47]*Ibid.*, p. 267.

[48]Henry Rutgers, Samuel L. Mitchill, Thomas Morris, "Report of the Commissioners superintending the Construction of a Steam Vessel of War,"

28 Dec. 1815, Montague Collection, Robert Fulton Mss, New York Public Library.

Robert Fulton and Naval Warfare

[1] Richard Knowles Morris, *John P. Holland, 1841-1914: Inventor of the Modern Submarine*, pp. 6, 31-32, 174.

[2] J.S. Barnes, *Submarine Warfare,* pp. 229-30.

[3] Samuel Colt, Fullers Hotel, Washington, D.C., to President John Tyler, Washington, D.C., 19 June 1841, reprinted in William B. Edwards, *The Story of Colt's Revolver: The Biography of Col. Samuel Colt*, pp. 160-61; also in Philip K. Lundeberg, *Samuel Colt's Submarine Battery: The Secret and the Enigma*, pp. 59-60.

[4] Colonel Joseph G. Totten, Washington, D.C., to Secretary of War William Wilkins, Washington, D.C., 1 May 1844, reprinted in Lundeberg, *Samuel Colt's Submarine Battery*, pp. 63-66.

[5] Colonel Joseph G. Totten, Colonel John J. Abert, and Lieutenant Colonel George Talcott, report to Secretary of War William Wilkins, 4 Feb. 1845, extract reprinted in Lundeberg, *Samuel Colt's Submarine Battery*, p. 56

[6] Taliaferro P. Shaffner, to the New York Historical Society, 30 Apr. 1856, Box 1B, Robert Fulton Mss, New York Historical Society.

[7] Donald W. Mitchell, "Admiral Makarov: Attack! Attack! Attack!"; Alfred P. Brainard, "Russian Mines on the Danube," pp. 52, 55-56.

[8] Richard Hough, *Admiral of the Fleet: The Life of John Fisher*, pp. 52-53.

[9] James MacGregor Burns, *Roosevelt: The Soldier of Freedom* (New York: Harcourt, Brace, Jovanovich, 1970), p. 250; Bernard and Fawn Brodie, *From Crossbow to H-Bomb* (Rev. ed., Bloomington and London: Indiana University Press, 1973), pp. 244-45.

[10] Samuel Eliot Morison, *"Old Bruin" Commodore Matthew C. Perry 1794-1858*, pp. 127-29.

[11] See Michael Orth, "The Stevens Battery," pp. 92-99.

[12] Admiral H.G. Rickover, "Nuclear Warships and the Navy's Future," p. 28.

Bibliography

SOURCES

1. Manuscripts, Correspondence, and Documents

Brannan, John, ed., *Official Letters of the Military and Naval Officers of the United States, during the War with Great Britain in the Years 1812, 13, 14, & 15*. Washington: Way & Gideon, 1823. 510 pp. Although it contains one important letter from Decatur concerning Fulton and naval warfare, this collection is generally disappointing.

Castlereagh, Robert Stewart, Viscount, *Correspondence, Despatches, and Other Papers*. Edited by Charles William Vane, Marquess of Londonderry. 12 vols. London: Henry Colburn and Others, 1850-53. Volume 5 was vital to this work, as it includes correspondence directly concerning the 1805 Boulogne raid, as well as Fulton's negotiations with the British government in 1805-06.

Decatur, Stephen, Mss. Naval Historical Miscellany, Library of Congress, Washington, D.C. 3 letters, 1752-1808. Of little help to this study.

Documents relating to the Claims of the Heirs of Robert Fulton. Privately printed, 26 Mar. 1840. Navy Department Library, Washington, D.C. 110 pp. Includes eyewitness accounts of Fulton's activities in the construction of the steam warship and troop transport.

Dumaine, J. and Plon, Henri, eds., *Correspondance de Napoleon Ier*. 32 vols. Paris: Henri Plon, 1858-70. Volumes 6 and 7 contain important documents concerning Napoleon's association with Fulton.

Farington, Joseph, *The Farington Diary*. Edited by James Greig. 8 vols. London: Hutchinson & Co., 1923-28. Illustrated, index. Very extensive and most useful memoirs by an English acquaintance of Fulton's. Includes several letters concerning Fulton's naval experiments in France.

Fitzpatrick, John C., ed., *The Writings of George Washington*. 39 vols. Washington, D.C.: Government Printing Office, 1931-44. Illustrated, index. The major printed collection of Washington's letters and other documents. Volume 35 contains letters concerning Fulton's canal projects in the 1790s.

Fulton, Robert, *Concluding Address on the Mechanism, Practice and Effects of Torpedoes*. Washington, D.C.: privately printed, 1810. 10 pp. An important speech, historically oriented and emotional, which attempts to relate Fulton's "torpedo" projects to the freedom of the seas.

——————————, Letters to the Right Honorable Lord Grenville. London: privately printed, 1806. 37 pp. A collection of original sources describing Fulton's work in underwater warfare.

——————————, Department of Special Collections, Columbia University Library, New York, N.Y. Approximately 20 letters, 1809-15, a 22-page manuscript "Thoughts on Free Trade," 9 Oct. 1797, and a copy of Fulton's *A Treatise on the Improvement of Canal Navigation*, 1796. Very important to this study, particularly the "Thoughts on Free Trade." Includes a copy of Fulton's letter of 5 Nov. 1814 to President James Madison requesting that Fulton be appointed secretary of the Navy.

——————————, Mss. Historical Society of Pennsylvania, Philadelphia, PA. One volume and approximately 50 letters, 1772-1815. This collection was very important to this work as it concentrates on Fulton's naval activities.

——————————, Mss. Library of Congress. Washington, D.C. One box, includes a rough treatise on submarine warfare and several letters, 1809-14. A disappointing collection. Treatise concepts may be found in Fulton's 1810 *Torpedo War and Submarine Explosions*.

——————————, Mss. New York Historical Society, New York, NY. Two boxes, approximately 200 letters, 1797-1843, and 5 volumes, 1811-1909. A major collection vital to this study. Covers a broad range of Fulton's naval activities, including his naval work in France and the United States.

——————————, Mss. New York Public Library, New York, NY. Nine volumes and one box, approximately 100 letters, 1790-1815. Along with that of the New York Historical Society, the most important Fulton manuscript collection. Particularly valuable for his European period and for his American "torpedo" experiments.

——————————, Mss. United States Naval Academy Museum, Annapolis, MD. Approximately 20 items, including letters, documents, and the original 1809 United States patent for Fulton's steamboat, 1798-1825. Most valuable for the Fulton-Decatur correspondence on naval warfare.

——————————, Mss. ZB File, Navy Archives, Washington, D.C. Miscellaneous letters relating to Robert Fulton. Of secondary importance to this study.

General Accounting Office, Congressional and Executive Letters Sent, Record Group 217, National Archives, Washington, D.C. Of secondary importance. Contains reference to Fulton's financial negotiations with the government.

General Accounting Office, Miscellaneous Letters Sent, Record Group 217, National Archives, Washington, D.C. Of secondary importance.

Hamilton, Stanislaus Murray, ed., *The Writings of James Monroe*. 7 vols. New York and London: G.P. Putnam's Sons, 1898-1903. Appendices, index. Contains an 1805 letter from Monroe to Madison that refers to a British complaint against Fulton.

Hunt, Gaillard., *The Writings of James Madison*. 9 vols. New York and London: G.P. Putnam's Sons, 1900-10. Index. A disappointing source. One must consult the Madison papers on microfilm in the Library of Congress.

Jefferson, Thomas, Mss. Library of Congress, Washington, D.C. Approximately 50,000 items, 1651-1826, on 101 reels of microfilm. Vital to this study and certainly the best single source for the extensive Jefferson-Fulton correspondence.

Koch, Adrienne, and Peden, William, eds., *The Life and Selected Writings of Thomas Jefferson*. New York: Random House, 1944. 756 pp. Index. Authoritative one-volume edition of Jefferson's major writings. Includes several hundred letters, some of which pertain to Fulton.

Lipscomb, Andrew A., and Bergh, Albert E., eds., *The Writings of Thomas Jefferson*. 20 vols. Washington: The Thomas Jefferson Memorial Association, 1905. Illustrated. A valuable edition, containing letters pertaining to Fulton and naval warfare.

Livingston, Robert R. and Family, Mss. New York Historical Society, New York, NY. Approximately 25,000 pieces, including books and letters, 1707-1880. A giant repository, the largest single collection in the New York Historical Society. Contains several pieces of correspondence with Robert Fulton.

Madison, James, *Letters and Other Writings of James Madison*. 4 vols. Philadelphia: J.B. Lippincott & Co., 1865. Index. Of very little help.

_____, Mss. Library of Congress, Washington, D.C. Approximately 11,550 items, including correspondence, memoranda, notes of dates in the Continental Congress and the Federal Convention of 1787, covering period 1723-1859, on 28 reels of microfilm. Very important to this study, as it is the best single source for the Madison-Fulton correspondence.

Mitchill, Samuel Latham, "Letters From Washington: 1801-1813." *Harper's New Monthly Magazine*, 58 (Apr. 1879), 740-55. Contains largely personal letters from one of Fulton's New York business associates.

"Nautilus," *An Address to the Senior Captains of the Navy*. Privately printed, 1834. 55 pp. A call for broad naval reform, by a person using the name of Fulton's submarine as a *nom de plume*.

The Naval Chronicle, 1799-1818. 40 vols. London: Joyce Gold, 1799-1818. A primary source of British naval activities during this period. Volume 20 contains a sharp denunciation of Fulton's activities in underseas warfare.

Navy Department, Record Group 45. M 209/4. Navy Department Library, Washington, D.C. Miscellaneous letters sent by the secretary of the Navy, 1798-1886. Microfilmed from the original sources in the National Archives. The basic source for correspondence of Secretaries Robert Smith, Paul Hamilton, and William Jones with Robert Fulton on naval matters.

New York Public Library, "Letters and Documents by or Relating to Robert Fulton," *New York Public Library Bulletin*, 13 (Sept. 1909), 567-84. Contains thirteen important original items, otherwise unavailable, about Fulton and his concepts.

Paine, Thomas, *The Complete Writings of Thomas Paine*. Edited by Philip S. Foner. 2 vols. New York: The Citadel Press, 1945. Index. Letters indicate a closer relation between Fulton and Paine than heretofore realized.

Perrin, W.G., ed., *The Keith Papers*. 3 vols. London: Navy Records Society, 1927-55. Index. Contains key papers of Admiral George Keith Elphinstone, Royal Navy. Volume 3 was very important to this work as it includes extensive correspondence relating to Fulton and the Boulogne raid, as well as to Fulton's other naval activities in England.

Rodgers, Commodore John, Microfilm copy of Mr. Frederick Rodgers's collection of John Rodgers's papers. New York Historical Society, New York, NY. Approximately 900 items on two reels, 1796-1835. Contains some sharp and revealing references by Rodgers to Fulton and his naval weapons in America.

Rodgers family papers, Mss. Library of Congress, Washington, D.C. 15,500 items, 1788-1944, Naval Historical Foundation Collection. The large repository includes little of value for this study.

Rutland, Robert A., editor in chief, *The Papers of James Madison*. Charlottesville, Virginia. Collection of Madison papers which includes a letter from Mrs. Joel Barlow to Dolly Madison concerning Fulton's bid in 1814 to become secretary of the Navy.

Sowerby, E. Millicent, ed., *Catalogue of the Library of Thomas Jefferson*. 5 vols. Washington: Library of Congress, 1952-59. Illustrated, bibliography, appendices, index. Very useful compilation of original Jefferson material not readily available elsewhere. Volume 1 particularly helpful.

State Department, Preliminary Inventories, E-807. Twenty-six documents pertaining to Robert Fulton, 1804-06. Record Group 59. National Archives. Official British naval records transferred to the United States

Department of State on 9 Mar. 1945, pertaining to Fulton's negotiations in England. Most important to this study. Includes several signed letters by Fulton, Castlereagh, and Melville.

Thornton, Mrs. William, "Diary of Mrs. William Thornton: Capture of Washington by the British." *Records of the Columbia Historical Society of Washington, D.C.*, 19 (1916), 172-82. Vivid description. Notes that Fulton was in town shortly thereafter.

Washington, H. A., ed., *The Writings of Thomas Jefferson.* 9 vols. Washington: Taylor and Maury, 1853-54. Index.Old but useful collection of Jefferson source material.

2. Public Documents

U.S. Congress, *American State Papers.* Documents, legislative and executive, of the Congress of the United States. Selected and edited under the authority of Congress. 38 vols. Washington: Gales and Seaton, 1832-61. *Naval Affairs*, 1, was vital to this study, because it incorporates Fulton's *Torpedo War and Submarine Explosions* and includes official reports on the *Fulton the First.*

U.S. Congress, *Annals of the Congress of the United States.* Vol. 27 (May 1813-April 1814). Washington: Gales and Seaton, 1854. Includes the provisions of the harbor defense act of 16 July 1813.

U.S. Office of Naval Records and Library, *Naval Documents Related to the Quasi-War between the United States and France.* 7 vols. Washington, D.C. Government Printing Office, 1935-38. Illustrated, index. Volume 6 contains an important letter describing Fulton's submarine operations in France.

3. Newspapers

National Intelligencer and Washington Advertiser, 1 Dec. 1806-30 Jan. 1807. Covers Fulton's return to the United States, as well as early activities in the nation's capital. Indicates a greater public appreciation of Fulton's naval weapons than of his steamboat.

New York Evening Post, 2 Jan. 1807-31 Dec. 1807. Best newspaper source for coverage of Fulton's historic 1807 steamboat trip up the Hudson. Indicates public much more concerned with the trial of Aaron Burr than with the steamboat.

Niles Weekly Register, 1811-15. Most useful for inclusion of both individual and editorial commentaries on Fulton and "torpedo" development.

4. Books, articles, book reviews, and unpublished studies

Allardyce, Alexander, *Memoir of the Honourable George Keith Elphinstone.* Edinburgh and London: William Blackwood & Sons, 1882. 432 pp. Illustrated, index. A compilation of primary sources which stress Keith's role in the raid on Boulogne and his views on Fulton's participation.

Baldwin, Hanson W., "Fulton and Decatur: An Unpublished Document." *U.S. Naval Institute Proceedings*, 62 (Feb. 1936), 231-35. A very important source, which emphasizes the close association between the two men.

Barlow, Joel, *Advice to the Privileged Orders in the Several States of Europe*. Ithaca: Cornell University Press, 1956. 116 pp. Originally written in 1792. The section entitled "The Military System" may have played an important role in the formulation of Fulton's naval ideas.

——————————, *The Works of Joel Barlow*. 2 vols. Gainesville: Scholars' Facsimiles & Reprints, 1970. Index. Of little help to this study.

Benton, Thomas Hart, *Thirty Years View*. 2 vols. New York: D. Appleton & Co., 1875. Illustrated, index. Animated reminiscences. Includes a warm eulogy to Commodore John Rodgers.

Bourrienne, M., *Memoirs of Napoleon Bonaparte*. 4 vols. London: Richard Bentley, 1836. Illustrated, maps, index. The recollections of Napoleon's private secretary to 1802. The best original source for Napoleon's derogatory comments about Fulton.

Clarkson, Thomas S., *A Biographical History of Clermont, or Livingston Manor*. Clermont, N.Y.: privately printed, 1869. Illustrated, appendix. Contains an important 1807 Fulton letter on naval command.

Colden, Caldwallader D., *The Life of Robert Fulton*. New York: Kirk & Mercein, 1817. 371 pp. Illustrated, appendices. Colden was Fulton's friend and first biographer. While the book is overly eulogistic, it is a valuable original source, containing more than one hundred pages of original letters in the appendices.

Crawford, A., *Reminiscences of a Naval Officer during the Late War*. 2 vols. London: Henry Colburn, 1851. Illustrated. An eyewitness account of Fulton's "torpedo" experiments in England.

Delpeuch, Maurice, *Les Sous-Marins a travers les siecles*. Paris: Societe d' edition et de publications, 1907. 480 pp. Illustrated, bibliography, appendix. A comprehensive French classic. Contains most of the Fulton sources held in the Archives Nationale.

Desbriere, Edouard, *Projets et tentatives de debarquement aux iles Britanniques*. 4 vols. Paris: Librarie Militaire R. Chapelot et Cᵉ, 1900-02. Contains original French documents relating to Fulton's naval activities in France, in particular, his attempt to interest Napoleon in the steamboat.

Fast, Howard, *The Selected Work of Tom Paine and Citizen Tom Paine*. New York: Modern Library, 1945. 640 pp. Contain's Paine's basic writings plus Fast's historical novel. Fulton's naval views are similar to those evinced by Paine in "The Rights of Man."

Fulton, Robert, *Report on the Proposed Canal between the Rivers Heyl and Helford*. London: privately printed, 1796. 15 pp. Map. One of Fulton's earliest published works, indicating his early preoccupation with canals in England.

——————————, *Torpedo War and Submarine Explosions*. New York: William Elliot, 1810. 60 pp. Illustrated, appendix. Fulton's major statement on naval warfare. Enhanced by his drawings of the various aspects and tactics of his system. Vital to this study. Also published in U.S. Congress, *American State Papers: Naval Affairs*, 1, pp. 211-27.

——————————, *A Treatise on the Improvement of Canal Navigation*. London: I. and J. Taylor, 1796. 144 pp. Illustrated. Fulton's most elaborate published work. Very impressively illustrated with scores of technical drawings by him. The general philosophy he expresses in the early pages of the book relates to his later thought on naval warfare.

Furber, Holden, "Fulton and Napoleon in 1800: New Light on the Submarine Nautilus." *American Historical Review*, 39 (Apr. 1934), 489-94. Contains two otherwise unavailable documents that indicate that Fulton's *Nautilus* was first launched and tested in Paris, in mid-June 1800, rather than in Rouen in July, as his major biographers believed.

Haswell, Charles H., "Reminiscences of Early Marine Steam Engine Construction and Steam Navigation in the United States of America from 1807 to 1850." *Transactions of the Institution of Naval Architects*, 40 (1898), 104-13. Text not relevant, but appended discussion notes include three Fulton letters on steam engines.

Herold, J. Christopher, ed., *The Mind of Napoleon: A Selection from His Written and Spoken Words*. Translated by J. Christopher Herold. New York and London: Columbia University Press, 1961. 322 pp. Appendix, index. Contains another translation of Napoleon's unflattering reference to Fulton.

Hunt, Leigh, *The Autobiography of Leigh Hunt*. 2 vols. New York: Harper & Brothers, 1850. Illustrated. Of secondary importance for the description of Fulton's London habitat.

May, Arthur J., "Stratford Canning on Shipping in America." *American Neptune*, 4 (Oct. 1944), 327-29. Brief but important contemporary European description of the *Fulton the First*.

de Montaut, Marie Josephine Louise de Navailles, duchess de Gontaut, *Memoirs*. Translated by Mrs. J.W. Davis. New York: Dodd, Mead & Co., 1894. 399 pp.

Munsell, J., "Steam Navigation on the Hudson." *The Annals of Albany*, 6 (1855), 2-45. One of the sources for Fulton's statement that he considered his naval weapons more important than the steamboat.

Owen, Robert, *The Life of Robert Owen Written by Himself*. 2 vols. London: Effingham Wilson, 1857. Appendices, index. Contains important observations about Fulton's personal qualities from an English companion.

Parsons, William Barclay, *Robert Fulton and the Submarine*. New York: Columbia University Press, 1922. Illustrated. An important source for its inclusion of several original documents on Fulton's second sojourn in England. The narrative portion lacks footnotes and bibliography, however, and its major thesis, that Fulton developed a radical new submarine, is challenged by this author.

Pasquier, Duc Etienne-Denis, *A History of My Time: Memoirs of Chancellor Pasquier*. Volume 1, 1789-1810. Edited by the Duc d'Audiffet-Pasquier, translated by Charles E. Roche. London: T. Fisher Unwin, 1893. 559 pp. Illustrated. These valuable memoirs of the chancellor of France describe the relations between Fulton and Napoleon.

Pesce, G.L., *La Navigation Sous-Marine*. Paris: Vuibert & Nony, 1906. 498 pp. Illustrated. The most important French work for this book, incorporating the Fulton documents pertaining to naval warfare that were located in the Archives Nationales in 1896.

"Robert Fulton's First Voyage," *Hunt's Merchants Magazine*. 15 (Nov. 1846-71) Along with Munsell, incorporates Fulton's statement on the relative importance of his naval concepts over the steamboat.

"Robert Fulton's Torpedoes," *Scientific American*. 78 (4 June 1898), 361. A brief account of the 1807 (incorrectly printed as 1806) "Torpedo" experiment.

Smith, Margaret Bayard, *The First Forty Years of Washington Society in the Family Letters of Margaret Bayard Smith*. Edited by Gallard Hunt. New York: Frederick Ungar Publishing Co., 1965. 424 pp. Illustrated, index. Pungent descriptions of Washington society during Fulton's residency at Barlow's Kalorama.

Stael-Holstein, Germaine, Baroness de, *Ten Years Exile*. Edited by Baron Augustus de Stael-Holstein. Fontwell, Sussex: Centaur Press, 1968, 434 pp. Illustrated. New edition of Madame de Stael's important observations of the European scene during Fulton's sojourn there.

[Strickland, M.] *A Memoir of the Life, Writings, and Mechanical Inventions of Edmund Cartwright*. London: Saunders and Otley, 1843. 372 pp. Appendix, index. This book is important, but must be used with caution. It is a rather odd blending of Strickland's comments, Cartwright's statements, and many original source letters, particularly those of Cartwright's friend, Robert Fulton.

Sutcliffe, Alice Crary, "The Early Life of Robert Fulton." *Century Magazine*, 76 (Sep. 1908), 780-94. Authoritative, personal account by Fulton's great-granddaughter. Incorporates some original Fulton letters not available from any other source.

——————————, "Robert Fulton in France," *Century Magazine*, 76 (Oct. 1908), 931-45. Fulton's great-granddaughter incorporates in this work some original documents of Fulton pertaining to naval warfare in France.

Todd, Charles Burr, *Life and Letters of Joel Barlow*. New York and London: G.P. Putnam's Sons, 1886. 306 pp. Illustrated, index. A most important source. Contains many letters between Fulton and Barlow relating to naval warfare.

Yarmolinsky, Avrahm, *Picturesque United States of America: A Memoir on Paul Svinin*. New York: William Edwin Rudge, 1930. 152 pp. Illustrated, appendix. The translated extracts of Svinin's memoirs of his stay in the

United States from 1811 to 1813. Contains Svinin's observations on Fulton's steamboat *Paragon*, as well as his role regarding Fulton's attempt to introduce the steamboat to Russia.

SECONDARY WORKS

Adams, Henry, *History of the United States of America During the Administration of Jefferson and Madison*. 9 vols. New York: Charles Scribners' Sons, 1889-91. Index. Classic account of America after Fulton's return. Although Adams makes an interesting correlation between Fulton's steamboat and the *Chesapeake* incident, he does not discuss Fulton's naval weapons.

Alberts, Robert C., *Benjamin West: A Biography*. Boston: Houghton Mifflin, 1978. 525 pp. Illustrated, bibliography, index. The most recent and best biography of West.

Albion, Robert Greenhalgh, *The Rise of New York Port, 1815-1860*. Newton Abbot, Devon: David & Charles, 1970. 481 pp. Illustrated, bibliography, appendices, index. Subject matter not limited to the time period indicated in the title. Contains helpful background on Fulton's New York waterfront setting.

Anthony, Irvin, *Decatur*. New York and London: Charles Scribner's Sons, 1931. 319 pp. Bibliography, index. Contains a brief reference to Fulton's steam warship.

Aubrey, Paul V., *Monge, le savant ami de Napoleon Bonaparte, 1746-1818*. Paris: Gauthier-Villars, 1954. 364 pp. Illustrated, appendices. French biography of the scientist who was involved in Fulton's French naval experiments. Of little help to this study.

Bacon-Foster, Cora, "The Story of Kalorama." *Records of the Columbia Historical Society of Washington, D.C.* 13 (1910), 98-118. A well-written account of Barlow's Washington estate, the base of Fulton's negotiations with key governmental figures on his naval weapons.

Barnes, J.S., *Submarine Warfare*. New York: D. Van Nostrand, 1869. 233 pp. Illustrated, appendices. An account by an American naval officer of the Civil War period.

Barlett, Christopher J., *Castlereagh*. New York: Charles Scribner's Sons, 1966. 292 pp. Illustrated, bibliography, index. Recent biography which ignores Fulton.

Bauer, K. Jack, "Naval Shipbuilding Programs 1794-1860." *Military Affairs,* 29 (spring 1965), 29-40. Intelligent synthesis that provides excellent background.

Baxter, James Phinney, *The Introduction of the Ironclad Warship*. Cambridge: Harvard University Press, 1933. 398 pp. Illustrated, bibliography, appendices, index. An excellent account of its subject, but contains only a passing reference to Fulton's steam warship.

Baxter, Maurice G., *The Steamboat Monopoly: Gibbons v. Ogden, 1824.* New York: Knopf, 1972. 146 pp. Bibliography, index. Contains a brief background on Fulton.

Bell, John F., "Robert Fulton and the Pennsylvania Canals." *Pennsylvania History,* 9 (July 1942), 191–96. Properly connects Fulton to the later development of canals in that state.

Bennett, F.M., *The Steam Navy of the United States.* Pittsburgh: W.T. Nichloson, 1896. 953 pp. Illustrated with appendices. Comprehensive but dated overview of the steam navy. Some reference to Fulton's steam warship.

Brainard, Alfred P., "Russian Mines on the Danube." *United States Naval Institute Proceedings,* 91 (July 1965), 51–56. Demonstrates Russians' effective use of mine warfare in the nineteenth century.

Brant, Irving, *James Madison: Commander in Chief, 1812–1836.* Indianapolis and New York: Bobbs-Merrill, 1961. 627 pp. Illustrated, index. Sixth and final volume of Brant's authoritative biography of the fourth president.

——————————, *James Madison: The President, 1809–1812.* Indianapolis and New York: Bobbs-Merrill, 1956. 540 pp. Illustrated, index. Fifth volume of Brant's definitive biography. Briefly considers but is unfavorably disposed to Fulton's 1810 "torpedo" test at New York.

Brown, 6 enneth L., "Mr. Madison's Secretary of the Navy." *United States Naval Institute Proceedings,* 73 (Aug. 1947), 967–75. A brief, generally laudatory essay on William Jones.

Burroughs, Alan, *Limners and Likenesses: Three Centuries of American Painting.* New York: Russell & Russell, 1965. 246 pp. Illustrated, index. This impressive survey of American art is very favorably disposed towards Fulton the painter.

Cable, Frank T., *The Birth and Development of the American Submarine.* New York and London: Harper & Brothers, 1924. 337 pp. Illustrated. Older, general account. Not well documented, and little detail on Fulton's work.

Calderhead, William L., "Naval Innovation in Crisis: War in the Chesapeake, 1813." *American Neptune* 36 (July 1976), 206–221. Contains a good account of Elijah Mix's "torpedo" activities in 1813.

Chapelle, Howard I., *Fulton's "Steam Battery": Blockship and Catamaran.* Washington: Smithsonian Institution, 1964. 29 pp. Illustrated, appendices. Reprinted from United States National Museum Bulletin 240. A basically technical account by the former curator of transportation at the Smithsonian Institution. Important for publication of lost plans of Fulton's steam warship which were discovered in Danish archives in 1960.

——————————, *The History of the American Sailing Navy.* New

York: W.W. Norton & Co., 1949. 558 pp. Illustrated, appendices, index. Comprehensive and authoritative. Contains hundreds of designs of naval sailing ships, as well as their specifications. Includes a detailed description of the *Argus*, the vessel used in Fulton's 1810 "torpedo" test.

Coles, Harry L., *The War of 1812*. University of Chicago Press, 1965. 298 pp. Illustrated, maps, bibliography, index. Excellent one-volume survey of the war. Very well written, but includes only one very brief entry on the *Fulton the First*.

Cowie, J.S., *Mines, Minelayers and Minelaying*. London, etc.: Oxford University Press, 1949. 216 pp. Illustrated, maps, bibliography, appendices, index. Excellent though brief one-volume survey of mine warfare. Although it does call attention to Fulton's role, it does not discuss this extensively.

Dangerfield, George, *Chancellor Robert R. Livingston of New York 1746–1813*. New York: Harcourt, Brace & Co., 1960. 532 pp. Bibliography, index. Definitive biography of Livingston. Includes one very useful chapter on Robert Fulton, which, however, concentrates on steamboats rather than naval warfare.

Dickinson, H.W., "Fulton in England." *Cassier's Magazine*, 33 (Apr. 1908), 602-13. This sketchy account does not develop Fulton's naval affairs in England.

_____, *Robert Fulton, Engineer and Artist: His Life and Works*. London and New York: John Lane Co., 1913. 333 pp. Illustrated, appendices, index. The major Fulton biography. Naval warfare, especially the American phase, not well developed.

Dunbar, Seymour, *A History of Travel in America*. 4 vols. New York: Greenwood Press, 1968. Illustrated, bibliography, appendices, index. Classic account, originally published in 1915. While most important for steamboat development, of negligible value for a study on naval warfare.

Duncan, Robert C., *America's Use of Sea Mines*. Washington, D.C., Government Printing Office, 1962. 173 pp. Illustrated, bibliography, index. A short overview of the history of mine warfare in America. Contains a basically sound but too brief six-page summary of Fulton's contribution.

Dutton, Charles J., *Oliver Hazard Perry*. New York and Toronto: Longman's Green and Co., 1935. 308 pp. Illustrated, bibliography, appendices, index. The major biography of the hero of the battle of Lake Erie. No mention of Fulton.

Eckert, Edward K., "Early Reform in the Navy Department." *American Neptune*, 33 (Oct. 1973), 231-45. Modern analysis of early naval administration. Pro-Secretary Jones and anti-Secretary Hamilton.

_____, *The Navy Department in the War of 1812*. Gainesville: University of Florida Press, 1973. 77 pp. Related to published articles by the same author. Concentrates on the role of William Jones. Well researched, with extensive footnotes.

_____, "William Jones: Mr. Madison's Secretary of the Navy." *The Pennsylvania Magazine of History and Biography*, 96 (Apr. 1972). 167–82. Authoritative, brief biographical sketch.

Edwards, William B., *The Story of Colt's Revolver: The Biography of Col. Samuel Colt*. Harrisburg: Stackpole Co., 1953. 470 pp. Illustrated, bibliography, appendices, index. The major biography of Fulton's successor in American mine warfare.

Emery, Fred A., "Washington's Historic Bridges." *Records of the Columbia Historical Society of Washington, D.C.*, 39 (1938), 49–70. Contains an account of the move to name Washington's P Street Bridge after Fulton because of his nautical experiments at Kalorama and on Rock Creek.

"The First Submarine Boat," *Scientific American Supplement*, No. 1345, 12 Oct. 1901. Very brief general essay on Fulton's French submarine.

Flexner, James Thomas, *Steamboats Come True: American Inventors in Action*. Revised edition. Boston & Toronto: Little, Brown, 1978. 406 pp. Illustrated, bibliography, appendices, index. This important book, originally published in 1944, is basically a history of steamboat development up through Fulton. While not a full-scale biography of Fulton, it does interweave the lives of the chief contributors to steamboat development. Contains a most useful bibliography and notes section.

Forrester, C.S., *The Age of Fighting Sail*. Garden City: Doubleday, 1956. 284 pp. Maps, index. The most interesting of all the naval histories of the War of 1812, as might be expected of the author of the Horatio Hornblower sagas. Very briefly mentions Fulton's naval weapons.

Glover, Richard, "The French Fleet, 1807–1804: Britain's Problem and Madison's Opportunity." *Journal of Modern History*, 39 (Sep. 1967), 233–52. Stresses Napoleon's naval buildup after his encounter with Fulton.

Gurley, Ralph R., "The U.S.S. Fulton the First." *United States Naval Institute Proceedings*, 61 (Mar. 1935), 322–28. Very brief but prescient technical appraisal before the Danish drawings procured by Chapelle were available.

Hagerman, George M., "Lord of the Turtle Boats." *United States Naval Institute Proceedings*, 93 (Dec. 1967), 66–75. An excellent account of the Korean warship that preceded the *Fulton the First*.

"A Half-Forgotten American Celebrity," *Tait's Edinburgh Magazine*, 27 (Apr. 1860), 215–18. A brief and curious mid-nineteenth century appraisal of Fulton from Scotland.

Hamlin, Talbot, *Benjamin Henry Latrobe*. New York: Oxford University Press, 1955. 633 pp. Illustrated, appendices, index. A masterpiece of biographical writing. Of all the biographers of subjects who had an important association with Fulton, only Hamlin, in company with Dangerfield and Woodress, has placed his subject in proper historical perspective with Fulton.

Hawke, David Freeman, *Paine*. New York, etc.: Harper & Row, 1974. 500 pp. Illustrated, bibliography, index. An excellent biography. Contains some references to Fulton and Paine's joint activities.

Herbert, Frederick D., "Robert Fulton's Original Drawings." *The Society of Naval Architects and Marine Engineers Transactions*, 42 (1934), 21–44. While potentially very important to any study of the steamboat, this piece makes only a slight reference to Fulton's steam warship.

Herndon, G. Melvin, *William Tatham and the Culture of Tobacco*. Coral Gables: University of Miami Press, 1969. 506. Bibliography, appendices, index. Useful to this study for its recounting of Tatham and Fulton's exchanges on canals.

Hill, Peter Proal, *William Vans Murray Federalist Diplomat: The Shaping of Peace with France, 1797–1801*. Syracuse: Syracuse University Press, 1971. 241 pp. Bibliography, index. Excellent background on the diplomatic scene in France during Fulton's first four years there.

Hindle, Brooke, *The Pursuit of Science in Revolutionary America, 1735–1789*. New York: W.W. Norton & Co., 1974. 410 pp. Illustrated, bibliography, index. Contains a succinct account of Bushnell's *Turtle*.

Hough, Richard, *Admiral of the Fleet: The Life of John Fisher*. New York: MacMillan, 1969. 392 pp. Illustrated, appendices, index. Judicious biography of England's foremost naval leader in the late nineteenth century. Connects his thought and development of the "torpedo" with Fulton.

Jordan, Douglas S., "Stephen Decatur at New London." *United States Naval Institute Proceedings*, 93 (Oct. 1967), 60–65. This short article conveys Decatur's frustration with the British blockade.

La Boeuf, Randall J., Jr., "Robert Fulton and the Fulton Ferry." *The Journal of Long Island History*, 10 (Spring, 1974), 7–20. More a good brief biography of Fulton than an in-depth study of his ferries.

Lee, Cuthbert, *Early American Portrait Painters: The Fourteen Principal Earliest Native-Born Painters*. New Haven: Yale University Press, 1929. 350 pp. Illustrated, bibliography, index. Considers Robert Fulton one of the "fourteen principal" early American portrait painters, in company with Copley, Stuart, Charles W. Peale, and Trumbull.

Lemon, James T., *The Best Poor Man's Country: A Geographical Study of Early Southeastern Pennsylvania*. Baltimore and London: John Hopkins Press, 1972. 295 pp. Maps, bibliography, index. Recent and scholarly demographic study of the scene of Fulton's childhood.

Lewis, Charles Lee, *The Romantic Decatur*. Philadelphia: University of Pennsylvania Press, 1937. 296 pp. Illustrated, bibliography, index. A highly readable biography, with the major thesis that Decatur was "one of the most romantic characters in American history." Contains a very brief reference to a friendly interchange with Fulton.

Long, David F., *Nothing Too Daring: A Biography of Commodore David Porter, 1780–1843*. Annapolis: United States Naval Institute Press, 1970.

396 pp. Illustrated, bibliography, index. Very well researched, with an excellent bibliography. No details of relations with Fulton.

Lundeberg, Philip K., *Samuel Colt's Submarine Battery: The Secret and the Enigma*. Washington: Smithsonian Institution Press, 1974. 90 pp. Illustrated, appendices, index. Recent succinct account of the underseas weapons development of Fulton's major American successor. Indicates that Fulton's work inspired Colt.

Mahan, Alfred T., *Sea Power in Its Relations to the War of 1812*. 2 vols. Boston: Little, Brown & Co., 1905. Illustrated, index. Classic account, which, surprisingly, does not mention Fulton.

Mahon, John K., *The War of 1812*. Gainesville: University of Florida Press, 1972. 476 pp. Illustrated, maps, bibliography, index. Recent narrative history of the war. Excellent background. Particularly judicious use of British Admiralty sources.

Malet, Hugh, *The Canal Duke: A Biography of Francis, 3rd Duke of Bridgewater*. London: Phoenix House, 1961. 200 pp. Illustrated, index. A brief but excellent biography of one of Fulton's major British benefactors.

Malone, Dumas, *Jefferson the President: First Term, 1801–1805*. Boston: Little, Brown & Co., 1970. 539 pp. Illustrated, bibliography, appendices, index. Fourth volume of this definitive study of Jefferson.

——————————, *Jefferson the President: Second Term, 1805–1809*. Boston: Little, Brown & Co., 1974. 704 pp. Illustrated, bibliography, index. Fifth volume of Malone's authoritative study of the third president. Malone cites the Jefferson-Fulton correspondence to some extent, but does not develop the implications to Fulton.

Meier, Hugo A., "Technology and Democracy, 1800–1860." *Mississippi Valley Historical Review*, 43 (Mar. 1957), 618–40. Imaginative and interesting essay. While Meier uses Fulton and his work as his first historical example of the association between technology and democracy, he does not discuss Fulton and naval warfare to any extent.

Miller, Perry, *The Life of the Mind in America: From the Revolution to the Civil War*. New York: Harcourt, Brace & World, 1965. 338 pp. Index. Although Miller died before he was able to complete this stimulating study, he did indicate that he believed Fulton was active before De Witt Clinton in promoting what was to become the Erie Canal.

Mitchell, Donald W., "Admiral Makarov: Attack! Attack! Attack!" *United States Naval Institute Proceedings*, 91 (July 1965), 57–67. Demonstrates the Russian naval interest in and their successful use of mines in the nineteenth century.

Morgan, John S., *Robert Fulton*. New York: Mason/Charter, 1977. 235 pp. Illustrated, bibliography, index. See Flexner comment on p. xviii of 1978 edition of *Steamboats Come True*.

Morison, Samuel Eliot, *"Old Bruin" Commodore Matthew C. Perry 1794–1858*. Boston: Little, Brown & Co., 1967. 482 pp. Illustrated, bibliog-

raphy, appendices, index. Distinguished biography of the "father of the steam navy."

Morris, Richard Knowles, *John P. Holland, 1841–1914: Inventor of the Modern Submarine*. Annapolis: United States Naval Institute, 1966. 211 pp. Illustrated, bibliography, appendices, index. An excellent biography. Morris gives Fulton more credit in submarine technology than did his subject.

New York Historical Society, *Official Robert Fulton Exhibition of the Hudson-Fulton Commission*. New York: New York Historical Society, 1909. 66 pp. Illustrated. This extensive program of the 1909 celebration of Hudson and Fulton's feats is valuable in that it references original sources in the hands of collectors as of that year.

Orth, Michael, "The Stevens Battery." *United States Naval Institute Proceedings*, 92 (June 1966), 92–99. Interesting account of the development of Robert L. Stevens floating battery. Weakened by failure to take Fulton's role into account.

Parks, E. Taylor, "Robert Fulton and Submarine Warfare," *Military Affairs*, 25 (Winter 1961-62), 177–82. The only study outside of this book to take into account Fulton documents released from the Admiralty in 1945, *q.v.*; however, as the length of this article indicates, the full significance of the documents is not developed.

Parrington, Vernon L., *The Colonial Mind*. Vol. 1 of *Main Currents of American Thought*. New York: Harcourt, Brace & World, 1927. 420 pp. Bibliography, index. Includes a short but beautifully written essay on Joel Barlow.

Patterson, Andrew, Jr., and Winters, Robert A., eds., *Historical Bibliography of Sea Mine Warfare*. Washington: National Academy of Sciences, 1977. 137 pp. Index. Excellent. Recent and comprehensive.

Paullin, Charles Oscar, *Commodore John Rodgers, Captain, Commodore, and Senior Officer of the United States Navy, 1773–1838*. Annapolis: United States Naval Institute, 1967. 434 pp. Illustrated, bibliography, index. Originally published in 1910, and still the standard reference. Indicates Rodgers's initial dislike of Fulton but does not develop their relationship further.

_____, "Naval Administration under Secretaries of the Navy Smith, Hamilton, and Jones, 1801-1814." *United States Naval Institute Proceedings*, 32 (Dec. 1906), 1289-1328. Old, but still useful for background. No mention of Fulton.

Perkins, Bradford, *The First Rapprochement: England and the United States, 1795–1805*. Philadelphia: University of Pennsylvania Press, 1955. 187 pp. Illustrated, maps, index. Standard reference. Contains only one brief notation of Fulton's steam warship, and none at all on his other naval contributions.

Pursell, Carroll W. Jr., *Early Stationary Steam Engines in America: A Study in the Migration of a Technology*. Washington: Smithsonian Institution Press, 1969. 152 pp. Illustrated, bibliography, index. Scholarly and well *written. Emphasizes, among other things, Fulton's important role in the field of engine manufacture. Includes a vivid description of his Jersey City engine shop, where he worked on the Fulton the First.*

Reigart, J. Franklin, *The Life of Robert Fulton.* Philadelphia: C.G. Henderson & Co., 1856. 297 pp. Illustrated. Although well illustrated, probably the least reliable of the Fulton biographies. No footnotes or bibliography.

Renwick, James, *David Rittenhouse & Robert Fulton.* Vol. 12 of *American Biography,* Edited by Jared Sparks, New York and London: Harper & Brothers, 1902. 193 pp. Illustrated. A later reprint of the early nineteenth century work. Rambling and discursive. Renwick appears to be more concerned with Rittenhouse than with Fulton. Material on naval warfare negligible.

Rickover, Admiral H.G., "Nuclear Warships and the Navy's Future." *United States Naval Institute Proceedings,* 101 (Jan. 1975), 18–24. A plea for a nuclear-powered navy, by the "father of the American Nuclear Navy," using as an historical example the slow development of a steam-powered navy following the launching of the *Fulton the First.*

Ridgely-Nevitt, Cedric, "The Steam Boat, 1807-1814." *American Neptune,* 27 (Jan. 1967), 5–29. Good background on Fulton's negotiations with the English government for his steamboat engine.

Rowbotham, W.B., "Robert Fulton's Turtle Boat." *United States Naval Institute Proceedings,* 62 (Dec. 1936), 1746–49. *Robert Fulton: Pioneer of*

Ringwald, Donald C., "The Beginning of Hudson River Steamboating²⁄₃ *American Neptune,* 20 (July 1960), 220–22. Brief but lucid description of Fulton's first American steamboat's early voyages.

—————————, "First Steamboat to Albany." *American Neptune,* 24 (July 1964), 157–71. A rather confusing but well-documented essay investigating the uncertain date of Fulton's first American steamboat voyage.

Robert Fulton Centenary Committee, "Report of the Committee of the Lancaster County Historical Society." *Lancaster County Historical Society Journal,* 13 (12 Oct. 1909), 193–221. Useful reminiscences of Fulton's birthplace.

Roland, Alex, *Underwater Warfare in the Age of Sail.* Bloomington & London: Indiana University Press, 1978. 237 pp. Illustrated, bibliography, index. A broad, comprehensive, well-researched, and imaginative overview of the key inventors in the field of underwater warfare from the sixteenth to the nineteenth centuries.

Roosevelt, Theodore, *The Naval War of 1812.* 6th edition. New York: G.P. Putnam's Sons, 1897. 549 pp. Appendices, index. More perceptive than most, Roosevelt gives Fulton credit for both the steam frigate and for his "torpedoes," but does not develop the subject.

Rose, John Holland, *William Pitt and the Great War.* London: G. Bell & Sons, 1911. 596 pp. Illustrated, appendix, index. Detailed and useful background, but no mention of Fulton's role in the war.

Rowbotham, W.B., "Robert Fulton's Turtle Boat." *United States Naval In stitute Proceedings*, 62 (Dec. 1936), 1746–49. *Robert Fulton: Pioneer of Undersea Warfare* disagrees with Rowbotham's major thesis that the Long Island Sound "Turtle Boat" was Fulton's.

Sellers, Charles Colemen, *Charles Willson Peale*. 2 vols. Philadelphia: American Philosophical Society, 1947. Illustrated, bibliography, index. Full biography, which does discuss, although not in detail, some of Fulton's activities.

Sleeman, C., *Torpedoes and Torpedo Warfare*. 2nd edition. Portsmouth, England: Griffin & Co., 1889. 354 pp. Illustrated, appendices, index. Denigrates all "torpedo" warfare before the Civil War.

Sprout, Harold and Margaret, *The Rise of American Naval Power 1776–1918*. Princeton: Princeton University Press, 1939. 398 pp. Illustrated, bibliography, index. This well-known study makes no reference to Fulton and naval warfare.

Stanhope, Ghita, and Gooch, G.P., *The Life of Charles Third Earl Stanhope*. London: Longmans, Green and Co., 1914. 286 pp. Illustrated, appendices, index. Old but excellent account, begun by Stanhope's descendant, but revised and completed by the eminent English historian G.P. Gooch after Ghita Stanhope's death. Considers Earl Stanhope to have been "the friend of Fulton."

Suplee, Henry Harrison, "Fulton in France." *Cassier's Magazine,* 32 (Sep. 1907), 405–19. Sketchy. Stresses steamboat development rather than naval warfare.

Sutcliffe, Alice Crary, *Robert Fulton*. New York: MacMillan, 1915. 195 pp. Illustrated. The second biography of Fulton by his great-granddaughter. Hampered by lack of bibliography, footnotes, and index. Little stress on naval warfare.

————————————, *Robert Fulton and the Clermont*. New York: Century Co., 1909. 367 pp. Illustrated, appendices, index. First and better of the Fulton biographies by his great-granddaughter. Most valuable for the inclusion of many family documents not otherwise available. However, lacks footnotes and bibliography, and makes almost no reference to naval warfare.

Taylor, George Rogers, *The Transportation Revolution, 1815–1860*. Vol. 4 of *The Economic History of the United States*. New York: Harper & Row, 1968. 490 pp. Illustrated, bibliography, appendices, index. Originally published in 1951, this book is considered a standard in transportation history.

Thurston, Robert, *Robert Fulton: His Life and Its Results*. New York: Dodd, Mead & Co., 1891. 194 pp. Illustrated, index. While this is probably the best nineteenth century Fulton biography other than Colden's, it is somewhat sketchy, lacks footnotes and bibliography, and does not address the subject of naval warfare to any extent.

Tolles, Frederick B., *George Logan of Philadelphia*. New York: Oxford

University Press, 1953. 362 pp. Illustrated, bibliography, index. An excellent biography. Notes the association between Logan and Fulton in France in 1798.

Tyler, David B., "Fulton's Steam Frigate." *American Neptune,* 6 (Oct. 1946), 253–74. A very well researched and very good technical account, although Tyler did not have access to the plans rediscovered by Chapelle. Does not discuss Fulton's relationship with Decatur.

Virginskii, V.S., *Robert Fulton 1765–1815.* Translated by Vijay Pandit. New Delhi: American Publishing Co., 1976. 221 pp. Illustrated, bibliography, appendices, index. Originally published in Moscow in 1965. Although overemphasizes Marx, contains a useful chapter on Fulton's steamboat developments in Russia.

Wagner, Frederick, *Submarine Fighter of the American Revolution: The Story of David Bushnell.* New York: Dodd, Mead & Co., 1963. 145 pp. Illustrated, bibliography, index. Brief but well written. Pro-Bushnell and anti-Fulton in tone.

Wheeler, H.F.B., and Broadley, A.M., *Napoleon and the Invasion of England.* 2 vols. London: John Lane Co., 1908. Illustrated, index. Comprehensive account. Basically considers Napoleon's judgment to be sound when he rejected Fulton's steamboat scheme.

"When Fulton Suggested Submarine Warfare." *Scientific American,* 115 (18 Nov. 1916), 458–59, 464–65. Sketchy account, with main theme being that the "unethical" nature of submarine warfare in Fulton's time was similar to that in 1916.

White, Leonard, *The Jeffersonians.* New York: Free Press, 1951. 572 pp. Index. A unique approach to the study of America's administrative history. Most helpful in providing background on the workings of Jefferson's and Madison's administrations.

Whittet Thomson, David, "David Bushnell and the First American Submarine." *United States Naval Institute Proceedings,* 68 (Feb. 1942), 176–86. Indicates that as Bushnell left France in 1795, he could not have met Fulton there.

————————, "Robert Fulton and the French Invasion of England." *Military Affairs,* 18 (summer 1954), 57–63. Although very short, this article includes a useful bibliography.

————————, "Robert Fulton's North River Steam Boat." *American Neptune,* 32 (July 1972), 211–21. Includes a "table of voyages" for Fulton's first American steamboat.

Winkler, John K., *The Du Pont Dynasty.* New York: Cornwall, 1935. 342 pp. Index. Indicates that Fulton in France played a role in the Du Ponts' move to the United States.

Woodress, James, *A Yankee's Odyssey: The Life of Joel Barlow.* New York: Greenwood Press, 1958. 347 pp. Illustrated, appendices, index. An excellent biography. Places Fulton in proper relation to Barlow generally, although Woodress considers Fulton somewhat of an opportunist.

Index

Addington, Henry, Lord Sidmouth, 63, 66
Adet, Pierre, 33–34
Allison, John, 75–77
Andre, John, 6
Andrews, Jeremiah, 7
Argus, 111–112, 114

Baldwin, Abraham, 31
Banks, Sir Joseph, 69–70
Barlow, Joel, 8, biography and publications; 19–27, 28, 34, 38, 40, 42, 44–45, 46, 52, 54, 58, 89, 90, 91–92, 93–94, 98, 100, 102, 104–106, 120
Barlow, Ruth, 23–25, 38, 44–45, 54, 90, 101, 120, 140–141
Barras, Paul, 37–38
Berkeley, George Vice Admiral, 1, 88–89
Betancourt, Augustin de, 151
Biddle, James, Commander, 130, 132
Bonaparte, Napoleon, 19, 39, 40, 41–42, 45–46, 49, 53–54, 59–60, 67–68, 73, 82, 118, 152
Boulogne raid of 1804, 73–79
Boulogne raid of 1805, 81–84
Boulton & Watt steam engine, 58, 65, 99

Bridgewater, Francis Egerton, Duke of, 11–12, 58
Brindley, James, 12
Brown, Adam, 130, 134–135, 137
Brown, Noah, 134–135, 137
Brownne, Charles, 100–101, 134
Bruix, Eustache, Admiral, 33–34, 39
Burke, Edmund, 22, 27
Burr, Aaron, 100, 114
Bushnell, David, 28–31, 35–36, 50–52

Caffarelli, Brest "port-admiral," 48, 52
Canning, Stratford, 139
Carey, Mathew, 15
Carnot, Nicolas, 32
Cartwright, Edmund, 10, 33, 38, 48, 58, 63, 69, 91
Castlereagh, Robert, Viscount, 66, 80–81, 86, 87, 89
Cavendish, Henry, 69
Chapelle, Howard, I., 135
Chauncey, Isaac, Captain, 110, 112, 126, 146
Chesapeake-Leopard Affair of 1807, 1–2, 88, 94, 107, 118
Clarendon, Lord, 71
Clark, William, 94

Clay, Henry, 117, 132
Clinton, De Witt, 115
Coast and Harbor Defence Company, 130, 132, 136
Cobbett, William, 75
Colden, Cadwallader D., 9, 35, 109, 130
Coleridge, Samuel Taylor, 12
Colt, Samuel, 150-151
Congreve, William, 69, 87
Copley, John Singleton, 8
Courtenay, William (Earl of Devon), 10-11
Crowninshield, Benjamin, Secretary of the Navy, 141-142, 146
Cutler, Manasseh, 21
Cutting, Nathaniel, 143-144

Dalton, John, 13
Dargast, Nathaniel, 47
Dearborn, Henry, Secretary of War, 2, 130
Decatur, Stephen, Captain, vi, 124-126, 127-128, 130, 132, 146
Decres, Denis, Admiral, 52
Delpeuch, Maurice, 36
Dorothea mine test, 84-86, 87
Drebbel, Cornelius, 28
Duer, William, 21-22
Du Pont, Eleuthere Irenee, 39

Ericsson, John, 152
Evans, Oliver, 56, 57

Farington, Joseph, 48, 63, 68
Fisher, John (Jacky), Admiral, 151
Fitch, John, 54-55, 57, 153
Flexner, James T., v
Forfait, P. A. L., 39-41, 46, 52, 59
Franklin, Benjamin, 7
Fulton, Harriet Livingston (Robert Fulton's wife), 24, 100-101, 148
Fulton, Mary Smith (Robert Fulton's mother), 4-5, 39

Fulton, Robert, 1807 threat to Royal Navy, 1-3; birth, 4; youth in Lancaster, 4-6; young artist in Philadelphia, 6-8; arrives in England, 1787, 8; personal characteristics, 7, 9-10, 23-25, 34-35, 39, 86, 91-92, 104-105, 109, 140; and canals, 11-17, 19, 25, 64, 102, 114-115; Canal Navigation, 13-15, 26; and steamboat, 11, 28, 53-61, 65, 99-101, 115-117, 151-152; Torpedo War and Submarine Explosions, 13, 68, 106, 108, 118, 150; and submarine Nautilus, 18, 28, 30-33, 39-50, 149-150; "To the Friends of Mankind," 26; "Thoughts on Free Trade," 27; "Motives for Inventing Submarine Navigation and Attack," 28; panorama, 38-39; as "Robert Francis," 64, 66, 70; and "Messenger," 68, 69; larger submarine design, 68-69; British contract of 20 July 1804, 72-73; and 1804 Boulogne raid, 73-79; and 1805 Boulogne raid, 81-84; Dorothea mine test, 84-86, 87; New York 1807 mine test, 2, 94-98, 151; and naval leadership, 101; New York 1810 mine test, 109-114, 125; steam ferry, 117, 134; camouflage, 119; "submarine gun," 124-126, 127, 149; steam warship, 126, ch. 5, 152-153; SECNAV bid, 140-141; Mute, 145-146, 149; patent fights 143-144; final illness and death, 146-148
Fulton, Robert, Sr. (Robert Fulton's father), 4-5
Fulton, Robert Barlow (Robert Fulton's son), 148

George III, 8

Gilpin, Joshua, 19, 37-38, 62
Goldsborough, C. W., 107, 108, 119
Grey, Charles, Earl (Lord Howick), 91

Hamilton, Paul, secretary of the Navy, vi, 105, 107, 108, 109, 110, 112, 114, 119
Hammond, George, 66, 70, 71
Hardy, Thomas, Captain, 122-123, 124
Harrowby, Earl of, 66
Hawkesbury, Robert, Lord (later Earl of Liverpool), 66
Henry, William, 54, 56
Holland, John P., 150
Hunley (Confederate submarine), 150
Hunt, Leigh, 9

Irving, Washington, 136

Jackson, Andrew, 144
Jay's Treaty, 18
Jefferson, Thomas, v-vi, 2, 10, 58, 96-99, 102-104, 108-109, 119, 120, 125, 127, 141, 149
Jones, Jacob, Captain, 130, 132
Jones, William, secretary of the Navy, vi, 119, 132, 133, 136, 137, 138, 140, 141
Jouffroy, Marquis de, 54

"Kalorama," Barlow's Washington home, 94, 104
Keith, George, Admiral, 73, 77, 79, 80
Key, Francis Scott, 69
Kittera, John Wilkes, Mr. and Mrs., 7

La Crosse, Rear Admiral, 82
Laplace, Pierre Simon de, 45, 46, 49, 50, 118
Latrobe, Benjamin, 121, 143
Lawrence, James, Lieutenant, 111, 112
Lear, Tobias, 15

Lewis, Meriwether, 94
Lewis, Morgan, Governor, 109, 130
Little Britain, Pennsylvania (Fulton's birthplace), 4
Livingston, Robert, 53, 56, 58-60, 65, 100-101, 103, 106, 109, 115
Logan, George, 34
Longstreet, William, 56
Lowndes, William, 132, 133

Madison, Dolley, 140-141
Madison, James, vi, 2, 60, 89, 104-105, 133, 136, 138, 140-141
Melville, Henry, Earl, 78, 79, 81
"Messenger" one-man submarine 68, 69
Mifflin, Thomas, Governor, 15
Mitchill, Catherine, 100
Mitchill, Samuel L., 100, 130
Mix, Elijah, 121-122
Monge, Gaspard, 33, 45, 46, 49, 50, 118
Monroe, James, 58, 65, 89, 119-120, 132, 139, 141, 143
de Montaut, Marie Josephine Louise de Navailles, duchess de Gontaut, 30-31, 71
Montgolfier, 33
Morey, Samuel, 56
Morris, Gouverneur, 115
Morris, Thomas, 130
Morse, Samuel F. B., 8
Murray, William Vans, 34
Mute, 145-146, 149

Nautilus, 18, 28, 30-33, 39-50, 149-150
Nelson, Horatio, Lord, 87, 122
Nepean, Sir Evan, 78
New York 1807 mine test, 2, 94-98, 151
New York 1810 mine test, 109-114, 125
North River Steam Boat, 99-101, 149

Owen, Robert, 12, 16-17

Paine, Thomas, 27-28, 59
Papin, Denis, 28
Parker, Daniel, 58
Pasquier, Etienne-Denis Duc, 60
Peale, Charles Willson, 7, 8
Peale, James, 7
Peale, Rembrandt, 39
Perrier workshop, 40
Perry, Matthew C., then Lieutenant, 153
Perry, Oliver Hazard, Commander, 120, 132, 134
Pinckney, C. C., 19
Pitt, William, 66-67, 70, 71, 80, 81, 84, 86, 87, 89-90
Playfair, William, 22
Pleville-le-Pelley, Georges, 32-33
Popham, Sir Home, 69, 71, 73, 79
Porter, David, Captain, 136, 137, 146
President—Little Belt incident, 107, 118

Quasi-War, 18, 34, 38, 107

Read, Nathan, 56
Rennie, John, 69
Revelliere-Lepeaux, La, Citizen Director, 32
Rickover, Hyman, Admiral, 32, 153
Rodgers, John, Commodore, vi, 107-112, 114, 118, 125, 126, 141, 146
Roosevelt, Franklin, D., 152
Roosevelt, Nicholas J., 56, 58, 117
Ross, John, 7
Rumford, Benjamin, 52-53
Rumsey, James, 54-57
Rutgers, Henry, 130, 148

Sachs, Alexander, 152
St. Vincent, Earl, 87
Sergeant, Nathaniel, 41, 53
Slater, Samuel, 65

Smith, Adam, 13
Smith, Robert, secretary of the Navy, vi, 103, 104
Smith, Sidney, Sir, 81, 89
Stael-Holstein, Germaine, Baroness de, 59
Stanhope, Charles, Earl, 11-12, 13, 16, 19, 37, 57, 62-63, 69, 118
Stevens, John, 56, 58
Stuart, Gilbert, 8
"submarine gun," 124-126, 127, 149
Sutcliffe, Alice Crary (Robert Fulton's great-granddaughter and biographer), 5
Symington, William, 56

Tatham, William, 16
Thayer, James, 38
Thornton, William, 143
Thrask, Israel, 42, 53
"Torpedo Act" of 1813, 120-121
Torpedo War and Submarine Explosions, 13, 68, 106, 108, 118, 150
Totten, Joseph G., Colonel, 151
Trumbull, John, 8
Turtle (Bushnell's submarine), 28-29, 35-36, 50
"Turtle Boat," 123, 128, 145
Tyler, David B., 129
Tyler, John, 150

Vanderlyn, John, 39, 54
Vatry, Bourbon de, 39
Verne, Jules, 32, 150
Villaret, Admiral, 48
Volney, M., 46, 49, 50, 118

Washington, George, 15, 33, 55
West, Benjamin, 8-9, 15, 16, 57, 101
West, Benjamin, Mrs., 9, 101
Williams, Helen Marie, 34
Wolcott, Oliver, 109, 130